Praise for *Collective Manifesta*

"There are some great books about personal manifestation and the law of attraction. *Collective Manifestation* shows us how to manifest dreams and goals through the power of a group. Melissa Wadsworth offers compelling ways to engage your personal power to create intentional communities that benefit our loving planet." **–Marci Shimoff,** Best-selling author of *Love for No Reason* and *Happiness for No Reason*

"Melissa Wadsworth takes community building and development to an entirely new level. Her clear and practical questions, tools, structures, and awareness exercises invite creativity and greater potential for both the individual and the collective. As individual members are empowered to bring their best, the community thrives. Understanding that form follows energy, Melissa shows the way toward energetic creation of productive and transformational communities. Thank you for this book!" **–Alan Seale,** founder of the Center for Transformational Presence^{SM} and author of *Create A World That Works* and *The Manifestation Wheel*

"In Melissa's inspiring work, we are given an opportunity to explore and envision a new way of creating and sustaining heart-centered communities. In a world that has developed to isolate individuals and fuel competitiveness, we need to envision blueprints for evolving new forms of community and restoring human cohesiveness and co-operation. *Collective Manifestation* helps us to envision, define and manifest structures for more enlightened living." **–Julie Umpleby,** founder of *Diamond Light World*

"Melissa Wadsworth's book *Collective Manifestation* is based on real experiences! This book, about manifesting group intention is a blessing to all who take the time to learn from it. Using the Akashic Records, her team of co-creators have assembled a "How to" of major proportions. Knowing about this book is useful for when you wish to create something. Owning and using this book will be a resource like your standard reference book that you'll come back to over and over again! Bravo." –**Maureen St. Germain,** Akashic Records expert, author of *Beyond the Flower of Life* and *Be a Genie*

"I love this book. It is describes an inspiring process for establishing an energetic foundation to community building. I know I long for a way to establish community that brings out the best in us and helps us to live in harmony with our earth and all life. This book gives us a blueprint for how we might begin to create such a community. Thank you Melissa for your wise words, your great heart and aspiring mind." –**Sharlyn Hidalgo**, author of *The Healing Power of Trees: Spiritual Journeys Through the Celtic Tree Calendar* and *Nazmy — Love is My Religion: Egypt, Travel and a Quest for Peace*

"How do we attain the community we want? Sometimes, if we cannot find it, we need to create it. This book inspires new ways of looking at community, new possibilities and inspirations that may leave you feeling motivated to create exactly the kind of community that would most satisfy you now, one you might not have imagined." –**Suzette Sommer,** social media activist

In *Collective Manifestation*, you will discover a template to build what your heart desires. Whether it's a community, a program, or a business, Melissa shares tools and meditation processes that will help you to begin the process and take it to a new level of awareness. What's particularly special in this template is that it begins with the energy - the yin process. Most of us are used to action - you make a decision, and go for it. With this book Melissa shows us the way to feel the energy of what is being called for us to create - not what we think should be created. Melissa has called on the collective consciousness to be the

driving force - no longer are we to do it alone. The power of our manifestation will evolve from co-creating our dreams with people we want
to be in community with. Thank you Melissa for sharing your vision of
a powerful process that will move us towards a new paradigm of community on our beautiful planet! **–Kris Steinnes,** founder of Women
of Wisdom and KrysalisLeadership.com

Other Works by Melissa Wadsworth:

Small Talk Savvy
The Small Talk Handbook (Kindle Edition)

Blocked to Brilliant
(digital course)

Web
www.melissawadsworth.com
www.collectivemanifestation.com

Blogs
Loving Manifestation
http://www.collectivemanifestation.com/blog

Manifesting Magic
http://www.melissawadsworth.com/blog

Collective Manifestation

GOLDEN
TORUS

SEATTLE, WA

Collective
Manifestation

Heart-Centered Blueprints
for Creating Intentional Community

Melissa Wadsworth

Golden Torus
Seattle, WA 98117

Printed in the United States of America

Library of Congress Control Number: 2014916166
Golden Torus

Wadsworth, Melissa

Collective manifestation : heart-centered blueprints for creating
intentional community / Melissa Wadsworth

Summary: "Ideas and processes helping individuals and groups to follow their dreams through creation of online and physical intentional communities, that inspire, innovate and contribute to positive social change and evolutionary realizations of love, peace and plenty around the globe." (publisher provided)

ISBN: 0990632008
ISBN 13: 9780990632009

1. Self-help 2. Social change 3. Spirituality
(paperback)

For all change pioneers . . .

who imagine the impossible,

befriend the unknown,

and happily offer their brilliance

to the world.

For all co-creators . . .

who make a great leap of faith

by simply believing in the power of people

to change the world

in the most surprising and magnificent ways.

Contents

Book One

Reception

Author's Preface

Engaging the Impulse to Create Heaven on Earth

I t's October 2012 and suddenly I am imagining heaven on Earth. I am envisioning what is possible. Not as a fantasy world, but as a community filled with unlimited joy and potential; an entirely different energy.

This new vision is the opposite of all the dark-future scenarios being portrayed in popular movies and being discussed in social media. These disheartening fantasies severely limit our imagination. Technologies advance only to keep humankind more enslaved than ever by dark forces refusing to relinquish power. Even in scenarios set hundreds of years from now, women are still being treated as objects to degrade; men are robot-like, having successfully been "raised" to subvert all inclinations of light. These are anti-compassion-empathy-love-joy-peace visions of anti-heroes and villains lazily rendered. Even the best of the future visions include war and the destruction of Earth's beauty and life. All this dominant darkness got me thinking about dreams that facilitate light and love.

For years I have dreamed of starting a retreat center for exploring personal growth, creativity and spirituality — a place of healing, beauty and easy exuberance. Then one day I was at the gym on the elliptical machine and a thought popped into my head: "**It's not a retreat center, it's a village!**" That simple shift in consciousness from individual desire to collective possibility changed everything.

A longing for a new community must have been percolating for a long while without my consciously knowing it. As a kid, I thought Disneyland looked like a good community to belong to. There were magical journeys, exciting adventures, tree houses and families that got along through humor and love — all of which excited the dreamer in me. This was a world I longed to inhabit. As a teen, I recall having the inkling that it would be cool to be an architect. Now I realize that this insight was a seed planted that would take many years to grow, evolve and take shape in an altered form — the form of offering energetic blueprints for new intentional community.

In my late thirties, I took the first steps to actually explore a new way of living. As I thought about purchasing my first home, I investigated and seriously considered becoming part of a co-housing project. In the end, due to the uncertainty of how long it would take the co-housing project to manifest, I bought a traditional townhouse. Still it was a home connected, rather than set apart from others, something that would continue to be important to me.

As timing is always perfect, this village inspiration arrived at a time when my own personal evolution made it possible for me to actively shepherd this vision — to let it flow through me. I understood finally that my life is a vehicle for divine light, which is always in service to something bigger than what my mental mind can imagine. I would not have dreamt it, but having received it, I can easily imagine the potential inherent in exploring what community can be.

As this inspiration got on my radar, I began to become aware of other community pioneers who have set out, mainly in the last twenty to forty years, to redefine what community can look like. Futurists like Buckminster Fuller long ago realized that we had barely scratched the surface of what was possible in terms of architecture, systems, innovations, sustainability and design.

What I have realized is that stepping into a new community vision is to live fully awake like never before, to be lit up — spirit, heart and mind. It offers fascinating and ongoing opportunities for learning about what others are doing, and for consciously participating in the evolution of collective consciousness. It offers the excitement of new beginnings, of operating from a new construct, and of developing trust in a process that unfolds answers and solutions innovatively and intuitively.

The group I have brought together from this spark of inspiration is called New Village 22. It is our intention that our community be a powerful anchor on this planet for creative expressions of love and joy, fruitfulness and harmony, curiosity and discovery, energetic collaboration and spiritual radiance.

Communities like this, created around the globe by people like you and me, will benefit individuals, collective humanity, and the entire cosmos. The high energy already being generated by countless people who have answered the call to co-create community is expansive.

Are you a community pioneer dreaming of manifesting a new way of living and interacting? Do you embrace the potential of communities online, in virtual realities, in your own town, or somewhere entirely new? Do you long to find where you most belong?

If you are called to take part in creating a new sense of community, whether you are three people or three thousand, this moment is ripe for you to engage your great potential with the brilliance of others. We are each a source of light that can be accessed and expressed in remarkable ways. We are each a wellspring of perfectly aligned interests, knowledge and skills that can complement and enhance the passions and experience of others. There is a choice to be made. Where we once sourced this brilliance individually, we are now being called to source brilliance collectively, to form an expanded and unified field of radiant possibility.

My greatest hope is that, one vision at a time, we expand what is possible for ourselves and for this beautiful planet we inhabit.

Are you ready to shift into your most loving and brilliant self? Are you willing to share your radiance and magnificence with an open heart as you become *one* with all hearts?

Now is the time to be filled with immense joy and a sense of infinite possibility like never before. It's time to tune into the energetic impulses to create for the good of all.

May each of you passionately express your talents and gifts without worry about whether or not there is a place in the world for someone like you. There is most certainly a place and a need for what only you have to offer. Occupy your life fully and you will find your community, your tribe. Engage your vision and you will know who to invite into the community you'd like to see in the world.

In love and radiance,
Melissa Wadsworth

Part I

PRACTICAL
CORE BLUEPRINTS

—⚬⚬⚬—

When we release our old ways in order to embrace
the unknown with an attitude of trust and wonder it
becomes the ride of a lifetime.
~ Zen Gardner

Introduction

The Conscious Hive

Let's build community based on healing, honey and harmony.
~ Sharlyn Hidalgo, author and Alchemical Healing teacher

S imilar to the concept of the hundredth monkey, where the collective shifts once a critical number of members embrace a new idea, I believe a domino effect is already in play around new versions of intentional community.

I wrote *Collective Manifestation, Heart-Centered Blueprints for Creating Intentional Community* to inspire the development of cohesive groups that will purposefully break from conformity, social programming, and status quo systems to address global issues, expand human potential, and explore new possibilities for living in the material world lit up from one's engaged heart and soul.

Part One of *Collective Manifestation* provides practical organizing blueprints that facilitate vision, focus and action. Each exercise is designed to help you clarify what your community will be (and not be), and how it will connect to the greater world. These processes are especially effective for the smooth initial creation of your community in terms of organization, communications, and authentic connection. This book is not strictly linear; it's multidimensional. There will be points when you'll be prompted to go to Part Two to pick up a specific intuitive tool that elevates your "playing-with-reality" ability.

The second part of *Collective Manifestation* offers intuition development processes that add an energy-play dimension to establishing an intentional community. This is the expansive part of community creation, building on the knowledge that everything is energy. These processes enable you to establish an intentional energetic foundation for your group. These processes are especially effective for empowering community intentions and connecting members to heightened creativity and problem solving, and to deeper learning and wisdom. Developing collective intuition is a portal to understanding sacred, energetic alignments.

Part Three of *Collective Manifestation* illustrates how the practical and intuitive processes merge to bring about intentional communities bursting with electric possibility. By the end of this book you will have a good understanding of the essential aspects of heart-centered collective manifestation. After many years of teaching the law of attraction and intuitive dream boards, I'm thrilled to be sharing blueprints for adapting these wisdom practices to the collective manifestation that is happening now.

Keep an open mind and open heart. The material that is meant to inspire you, will. This book is not about one right way to form the best community for the 21st century. It's about utilizing the brilliance of your mind and heart in new ways. It's about shifting into inspired authentic expression and expansion for the good of self and others. Use what resonates and fits your particular community goals.

Of course, someone must be willing to engage group members in the exercises presented here, and to keep track of your progress. If you are the leader of your new community, that person is you. This book is designed to help make this a simple process. Don't overcomplicate. Remember this is new community, not a copy of old, red-tape, over-processed community. Believe that it can all unfold more easily than anything you have ever done.

Follow your allied hearts, and spirit-driven creativity, in honor of the belief that the time for collective brilliance is now. Each person has genius to contribute to help pollinate new projects and outcomes for the benefit of all. Let's move toward the realization of heaven on earth.

Thank you for saying "Yes" to this opportunity. Welcome to new community. You were always meant to arrive here. Your inner home beacon has brought you this far and will continue to guide you perfectly.

Chapter 1

What Is New Intentional Community?

*Community means strength that joins our strength to do
the work that needs to be done... A circle of friends.
Someplace where we can be free.*
~ Starhawk, author and social activist

The process of refreshing the concept and purpose of community has recurred throughout human history. Over the past two or three decades, much of what is innovative in community revitalization has flown under the radar of the general public. Where there has been structural decline and widespread depersonalization in many mainstream or generic communities, innovation and deep connection characterize more experimental communities. From the co-housing and ecovillage movements, to online communities, and worldwide spiritual and societal laboratories, intentional communities are shaping a new world reality.

These purposeful communities seek ways to thrive through shared vision and daily focus. They encourage sharing one's life, one's presence, and one's gifts in a larger context than personal gain. Rather

than fix what is unworkable in current community, the trend is to begin anew with intention, devotion and dedication to what a committed group of individuals can create when they are inspired, fully engaged, and purposeful. Are you ready to shift into this new perspective
of connectedness?

It is easy to argue that community in much of the United States is
made up of disconnected elements that have lost any sense of shared
context. We are in residence, rather than being in community. This
stems from an outward societal focus on consumption — how much
can I acquire, buy and own. Yet, such an outward focus does not nec-
essarily promote neighborliness or true personal connections, just as
convenience does not fill us up in any true meaningful way.

Have you felt it — how we've have lost the sense of shared connection that comes from sharing our inner brilliance? Individual goals and
greed splinter community cohesiveness. Social isolation is pervasive.
Whether or not we interact with one another seems a factor of casual
friendliness rather than deeper or higher purpose. Engagement with
others is often filled with perceived societal expectations rather than
with the intention and desire to know others. When I lived in Princeton,
New Jersey, in the late 80s, people left their townhouses in the morning for commutes to New York or Philadelphia, and returned at night
without having had any interaction with neighbors. As a single person,
I found few opportunities to take advantage of the beautiful location in
the company others. So I left as soon as I could.

There are exceptions, of course. There are close-knit communities
that support members and bond together during times of challenge.
They generally know each other's life stories or at least about current
living situations. The best communities create reasons for individuals
to gather, to share of themselves, and to receive meaningfully from one
another.

Right now we have the opportunity to take our natural inclination
to be part of something bigger than ourselves to expansive new heights.

Something new is emerging: active communing that lovingly serves individuals, local populations, and the greater world of all living beings.

New essential communing

Creating new community is tapping into what it means to commune at this point in human history. What is possible? What is desired? What structures help us to leap forward in a healthier relationship to Earth? What values facilitate a more engaged connection to daily life for people of all ages? What discoveries and inventions arise from communing with spirit as the foundation of creation?

Those who are being called to create new community are utilizing a broad spectrum of perspectives, interests, skills and resources to do so. For some, the alluring possibilities inherent in technology lead to innovation related to what is possible online and in virtual worlds. Others are strongly inspired by what is possible in terms of architectural forms that facilitate the effective functioning of new community. There are those who are called to rebel against current societal limitations in order to create societal structures that are more inclusive and more reflective of current lifestyle choices and values.

We are each responsible for the reality we call into being individually and collectively. Essential communing amplifies what we can be, do and create as individuals who choose to join as a unified force. The basis of new intentional community is a fresh realization that we are connected rather than separate beings. This realization is showing up in fascinating and amazing ways, as more individuals break free from limited thinking, acting and being.

Essential communing strengthens our resolve to lead life from the heart-mind (love-based heart wisdom and knowing in the moment) rather than the ego-mind (comparison-based mental judgments and fear). Many, if not most, of us have been taught to put our brains in charge and to question the wisdom of the heart. So it is quite a shift to lead from the heart in a truly trusting manner. Yet, this is how we can begin to manifest a balanced reality, how we can harmoniously co-create with our wonderful minds.

Essential communing is about authentic relationships transpiring in common and surprising fashions. In today's intentional communities you will find lively engagement and support whether it's ongoing, project-based, or found in periodic conversations. You will discover people stepping out of traditional roles to inhabit roles that didn't exist ten years ago. You will notice people asserting their personal flair as part of a team effort. It's an opportunity to expand one's sense of self and to play with manifestation in a grander framework.

New community is the opportunity to create space where mind, heart and soul align progressively. Life-long community participant Suzanne Anderson describes communing as a "deep conversation, as a challenge to grow and develop."

To come back to the essence of community, there is a need for shared goals, values and vision that energizes and engages the whole, while generating an atmosphere of belonging and love. The first part of this book offers tools and exercises for facilitating such a shared context.

Within refreshed community, we can connect to our creator-healer-always-learning selves by acknowledging, sensing and bonding more deeply with the sacred energy that is always present for us. The second part of this book will present tools and processes for expanding intentional energy in order to manifest more creatively and intuitively.

Collective manifestation shift:
From exclusive to inclusive community

In the past, community was a place of security. Over the past fifty or so years we saw the rise of gated communities and other exclusionary enclaves focused on security for a few rather than on peace and prosperity for the whole. Now we are shifting from "I" to "We" in a new form. Today's "We" is not just about taking care of one's immediate community; it's about having a ripple effect in the wider world.

New community is not about everyone being the same or fitting some kind of idealized profile. Inclusiveness is about allowing for authenticity. It's about playing with how different perspectives, inclinations, and personality patterns can benefit the whole. It's about each person owning their leader self. No two communities can be exactly the same. Each intentional community is comprised of members with individual gifts and goals. Each community is a hive for specific activity and pollination.

If you look at how society's collective comfort zone keeps getting challenged you begin to appreciate that, even when we don't choose inclusiveness, it happens anyway. There's no way to prevent consciousness expansion. In the modern era, the social and political rights of minorities challenged majority structures and practices. Affirmation of gay rights segues into acceptance of transgender rights. In education, dyslexia appeared as a non-conforming learning style and was quickly followed by ADD, ADHD, and autism — all of which challenge us to adopt and accept new ways of learning. Minority spiritual practices, like Wicca and Paganism, challenge societal myths and narrow views of what spirituality is and how it shows up as rituals and practice.

In every area of life we are presented with people who are here to turn these social norms on their heads. Inclusiveness is not about fixing other people; it's about making room for what they uniquely offer society and the world. It's about giving each person the space to find their own remarkable way to contribute. Humanity will continue to successfully navigate life on Earth not because we've managed to corral and limit the diversity of human expression, but rather because human potential expands whether we like it or not.

I believe today's intentional communities welcome differences — integrating them in exciting ways rather than expecting assimilation. And communities will increasingly have the desire to actively connect and collaborate with other communities. I envision networks of communities interacting in remarkable ways that nourish the whole world. Each group is essential to, influences, and supports the big-picture global community that we are co-creating.

Intentional community includes any group that connects in order to influence and further human potential and positive global change. This might be athletes expressing physical potential, healers advancing healing modalities, gardeners creating urban oases, and supportive parenting forums. By linking together in meaningful ways, activists amplify their efforts, creatives expand and elevate expressions of public art and entertainment, researchers establish more effective ways of complementing each other's work, and independent entrepreneurs provide vital support, feedback and social connection for one another, and much more.

So while we haven't broken completely free from the constructs of old social programming, we are giving ourselves permission to explore what it means to *belong*. More than ever, you have more options for belonging, for bringing back a sense of connectedness into your life, for living bravely and exploring new community terrain.

Physical intentional community

There will always be intentional communities that manifest at geographical locations around the world, like the Damanhur Federation in Northern Italy and the Findhorn Ecovillage in Scotland. This includes the many co-housing, agricultural, environmental and spiritual communities scattered around the globe. These communities attract people who want, in varying degrees, to immerse themselves in a shared-life experience. There is something singularly satisfying in bringing vision and lifestyle ideas into physical manifestation this way. These physical communities help embody heart-energy on our planet through daily communing, ceremonial rituals, physical structures, and a close relationship to nature and to the spirit of the place they occupy.

Intentional community includes groups that come together for special events in order to bring awareness to changing social, spiritual and cultural dynamics, and to provide periodic learning forums. Several years ago I co-founded a group called "Women Embracing Change" with four other women. Rather than individually trying to lead seminars and workshops focused on helping women in midlife deal with personal and business challenges and changes, we joined together to do so. This enabled us to share the work of putting events together and to offer participants a broader range of topics for discovery on an ongoing basis. What could have been a hassle for one person really became a fun growth opportunity and community adventure for the five of us, based on our sharing the value of learning.

Such event-based communities shine an inspiring light on emerging areas for personal growth and collective wisdom expansion. They allow people to unite with clear intention. The success of the TEDx events is a great example of the global response to open-hearted conversation and the exchange of ground-breaking ideas. Truly, the potential for intentional communities to do amazing things in the world is unlimited. No longer do you need to go it alone or to be isolated. In fact, going it alone is passé, part of the old paradigm. It's easier than ever to connect with others who desire the social rewards of community. And all around you are opportunities to contribute your energy to a committed group of people who have great ideas and passion, and who generously share what they know.

Online intentional community

Today's intentional community also includes the growing number of groups that meet online, in social media, through blog feeds, coordinated remote events, and even in virtual worlds. These online communities create energetic hubs for specific focus, discussion, and learning. The online format makes it simple to engage and initiate with others. This layers life in a meaningful way that was unimaginable before the advent of the World Wide Web, blogging popularity, and the explosion of social media.

Award-winning Indian documentary filmmaker and digital creative director Raja Choudhury of Delhi is a successful online community leader. Ever since his days in architectural school in the 1980s, he has been able to envision communities existing in cyberspace. Yet, until technology catches up with the 3D structures needed to support his particular vision, he channels his desire for meaningful community into social media. He founded "Spirituality and Consciousness" on the social media website LinkedIn five years ago. It currently has more than 7,600 members comprised of life coaches, healers, and healing businesses.

According to Raja, online groups hold the potential for amazing collective outcomes. "At the strictly materialistic level there is a high to seeing the number of members climb each day and to see the stats of people using the community. At the next level is the sense of community — the etiquette, friends you make, words of wisdom that comfort you, group support, group therapy and ideas. This is good for healing and avoiding the loneliness and aloneness of the spiritual quest."

Raja shares that at another level cohesive groups can mentally, emotionally and spiritually shift a large number of people all at once. "Every once in a while a nugget of wisdom blows through one of the discussions and hundreds of people are affected. You never know what wisdom will come, what ideas will emerge, what new thoughts may just change your life. It is quite wonderful to see enlightenment and spiritual companionship evolve in unusual ways amongst members."

Social media activist Suzette Sommer also believes that social media is a great way to connect with people who have similar dreams, hopes, concerns and commitments. With nearly four thousand worldwide followers on Facebook, she focuses on connecting to others through political and social-change topics. "Finding each other in this world is validating and encouraging — to know that we are not alone; to realize what we have in common with many people worldwide."

Researchers are looking at the rise of community in virtual worlds such as "Second Life." Jessica Falcone, assistant professor of sociology, anthropology and social work at Kansas State University, has studied the practice of Buddhism on Second Life. What she has observed is that participants use the virtual world to replicate what happens in the physical world — meditation, and participation in religious events. They also gather virtually to complement their real-world practice.

New intentional community is flexible. My own group envisions a future physical representation of the remote group we currently are. Once you are able to break free from your ego dictating the outcomes, and can open up to what wants to appear through heart guidance, the possibilities explode. You can assemble community in one format that meets current needs and transition to another form if appropriate or helpful. It's all about the intent and desire of the collective manifesting the community reality.

Each of these community options layer life with new dimensions of possibility for connection, experience and innovation. For each individual coming into such communities, the question is: "What will you do with the opportunities you have to connect to others, and how will you create the world of your dreams?"

Collective Manifestation Blueprint Exercise: Defining Your Community

I recommend that you keep a notebook or online journal to help consolidate the clarity you receive from engaging the exercises in this book.

1. To help define your community, answer the following questions:

   * What kind of community do you wish to create or take part of?

   * What is the best form and function of your group? Here are some questions you can use to facilitate the conversation with your community.

     → Are there immediate agreements about what form your group will take?
     → Will you be a project-based community that unites only for specific projects?
     → Are you an online group?

→ Do you connect in person?

→ Are you a residential or business community? Or other?

→ How do you or will you meet up — through discussions, project work, volunteer projects, remote assignments, in person?

→ Would using existing structures/buildings/homes help to establish your community? If "Yes" who could you align with to do this?

→ Is a specific environment necessary for your central community focuses?

→ Do you have a schedule and deadlines for your work or are you more loosely organized?

✳ How does (or will) your group or community practice inclusiveness? What inclusiveness is important to you?

✳ What is your community purpose?

→ **Community leaders/organizers**: *What is, or will be, the purpose of your community?*

→ **Community members:** *If you are interested in joining a community effort, what purpose would attract you to it?*

→ **Leaders and members**: *Why is this purpose important to you? What difference might it make in the world?*

2. Review your answers and create a brief description (1-3 sentences) of your community.

3. Create an invitation for others to join you. What would it say?

Chapter 2

The Creator Heart

All friendly feelings for others are an extension
of a man's feelings for himself.
~ Aristotle

T oday's groups and communities are not in the mold of the communes of the 1960s and 1970s. There are pivotal differences,
with the most important being that the individual is meant to
shine within the supportive atmosphere of the collective, not merge
into a homogenous unit. In the past, it was more common to be expected to leave your individual aspirations at the door in order to contribute to the good of all. Today, online and face-to-face communities
are learning how to best funnel individual inspiration, focus and drive
through heart-centered cooperation and collaboration. Individual brilliance is not suppressed or lost; it is celebrated.

The world needs all the star-power of each individual that can be
accessed, utilized and expanded. More than ever we need to reexamine
concepts of personal worthiness so that we might participate with more
personal confidence and generosity of spirit.

The best of the new intentional community will provide opportunities to develop the self, while contributing to others. What is valued
in intentional community is mutual focus, clear intentions, avenues of

safe expression, and outlets for an array of talents, interests and skills that facilitate lively engagement in the physical world. Not knowing exactly what treasures will come out of interactions is acceptable.

From the people that I spoke with both leading and participating in groups and community, I learned there is less desire for everyone to think similarly. Diversity of perspective is valued for helping to keep discussions open and generative. You don't need to give up your individual identity and desires in order to endorse heart-based groups as effective forces for change.

Already diverse communities present many choices for aligning one's initiative — whether it's expressed as ideas, inventions, activism, physical excellence, creativity, Earth stewardship, humor, healing, or spirituality. It may seem counter-intuitive that by joining with others you can become your best and brightest self. Yet, many of today's online and physically-situated communities actively encourage members to meaningfully step up and speak out authentically.

I watched a TEDx University of Nevada presentation titled, *Hackschooling makes me happy.* A young teen named Logan LaPlante explained to the audience how community plays a big part in his unorthodox education. This was evolutionary on so many levels: the child teaching the adults; the younger community member confidently presenting his break-out perspective; the adults appreciating the wisdom of the teen actively creating the education system he wanted, and the child refusing to buy into the belief that earning a living is more important than having a happy life.

This kind of nonconformist inspiration is key to creating an open-hearted, non-hierarchical atmosphere that invites active participation by all. New intentional community is no longer developed through the filter of paternalistic guidance. Individual potential is engaged at a high level while one learns from and collaborates with others. It's an exciting attitude of "let's break free," which leads to breakthroughs and the revolutionary concepts and solutions we need.

Heart-centered community is where your presence is celebrated and valued. Artist, international teacher and non-profit organizer Erin

Lee Gafill has deep family roots in the small community of Big Sur, California, where her family founded the famous Nepenthe Restaurant. She learned from her grandmother Lolly that it was okay to try anything and to be anything. It was only as an adult that she realized most people did not get this message. So Erin infuses her communities with the message that it's "safe to be your wonderful being."

In 2010 Erin and her husband Tom toured the United States offering free art programs for children of all ages, which gave them great insight into how much hunger for self-expression and beauty exists in America. Erin's live and online groups (one for painting and creativity, and another for writing) are imbued with her strong cherishing of people. "I'm anti-critiquing and tearing down," she emphasized. "I create safety for self-expression. My method is exploration and doing. Creating a mess is acceptable. I get turned on by tapping into this world of creativity, which leads to more creative thinking and growth. Everyone deserves to feel connected to their creative spirit." Erin is a great example of the creator-heart that is being expanded in the world community.

Intentional communities are ideal for bringing the energy of many willing hearts into alliance as a remarkably creative and welcoming force. A simple view of community is people with shared values sharply focused on common goals. The big-picture vision is multi-dimensionally aligned individuals initiating healthy and holistic planetary changes and manifesting remarkable advancements that benefit many like never before. To empower individuals to this level of engagement and achievement, we need to make the shift from consumer to creator.

Collective manifestation shift: From consumer to creator

Even as we have been socialized to stand out and succeed, we have increasingly seen the gap widen between the haves and the have-nots. Could it be that the trance of consumerism is actually a distraction keeping you from your true brilliance? Waking up from this trance is to realize that what you earn and spend may not be directly linked to your life purpose, your true talent, your unique skills and experience, or your intuitive gifts.

In the past decade, the popularity of the law of attraction gained attention as a way for individuals to take charge of intentional manifestation and create the life of their dreams. The upside has been that by understanding that energy attracts like energy, more people have come to understand how mental dialogue and subconscious beliefs can either empower or block desired manifestation. Yet, still trapped in our identities as consumers this wisdom has been applied by many people as: "How can I consume more?"

It's time to shift our manifestation abilities. First we need to see the extent to which we have been programed to believe in purchasing power, not people power. We need to perceive ourselves as creators rather than consumers. It's important that we want to see ourselves as something more; that we believe we deserve more. Only then can we truly step into our co-creator power and say goodbye to our old identities.

This doesn't mean you have to live without things or comforts. It means self-identifying differently, aspiring differently, dreaming differently, and being in the world with a new sense of belonging that is not based on how you look, or what you buy. It is based on what you bring forward from your authentic presence, from your willingness to share your skills, gifts, talents and interests; from your eagerness to initiate and engage life fully awake and alive.

There are numerous points that I could highlight showing the difference between the old and the new paradigm. For the purpose of this book, the following points relate most directly to the energy of emerging community.

Old consumer paradigm:

* Look outside yourself for what you need, your solutions, your things, your place, your role, your qualifications, your BE-long-ing-ness.

* Define your individuality in limited terms (roles, titles, life phases).

* Mental, ego-driven and competitive (what I have/lack, achieve/ fear defines me).

* Longing to be special, to standout (appearance, wealth, accom- plishments, special skills and abilities).

* Focus is on how to make things happen in the seen world for the good of one's individual life.

* Desire to fit into the prevailing societal structure.

* Time based in the past and future.

New creator paradigm:

* Look within self for the genesis of what wants to flow through you and for your connection to all.

* Realize that you are an unlimited aspect of divinity.

* Heart-driven creative enthusiasm in alignment with soul mis- sion.

* Longing to elevate the collective through abilities, interests and actions.

* Primary focus is on a balanced and co-creative energy exchange with others for the good of all.

* Desire to go *beyond* the status quo.

* In the now moment.

What you choose to create doesn't have to make sense to your logical mind. Like Logan, you can choose to create just because it makes you happy, just because you can.

Collective Manifestation Blueprint Exercise: Attracting Your Community Co-Creators

So who are you joining with to realize your vision, to change the world, to get more enjoyment out of life? Once the idea of a village percolated in my mind for a month or so, I chose to invite two people who have complementary, yet distinct skills, perspectives and life experiences. Both Gabriele and Paula are open-hearted women with quite remarkable minds. Gabriele lives in Europe, and Paula lives in the Seattle area. As a group that meets remotely and online, I love that we can create across the globe and that physical distance matters not at all.

Almost immediately upon joining together we discovered that group members do not have to participate in exactly the same manner. Although my role is that of the leader and organizer, other members are free to take leadership or organizational initiative. We have realized that when one member cannot participate in a scheduled meeting or event her energetic presence remains vital to the process. It is a fluid and dynamic system.

Who would you like to join you in creating new community? Like our group, you can start small and add members as you are inspired to, or you may immediately know of a larger group of people that you would like to invite.

1. Some preliminary questions to ask yourself:

    *   Who has skills that complement yours and the purpose for your community?

    *   Who do you want to work with because they light you up?

    *   Who has gifts and talents needed for your vision of community?

* Who do you know that is looking for more meaningful engagement in life?

* Who has suddenly appeared on your radar as someone you'd like to know better or talk to about this community possibility?

* Who do you believe would commit to such a project?

* Do members need to commit or is coming into and out of the group okay at key junctures (meditation foundation, design stage, implementation phase)? What would be the minimum commitment?

* What will be the structure of your group? Will you always lead the process or will members take turns? Can you be flexible with this?

2. Name 2-8 people you would like to initially invite and why. Let your intuitive guidance inform these decisions. What you notice matters. Be alert to what you notice about your interactions with people of interest. Trust that you can't get this wrong once you set the intention to become aware of and invite the people that will help you simply begin this project.

Name	**Why**
1.	
2.	
3.	
4.	
5.	

6.

7.

8.

Collective manifestation shift:
From mental dictatorship to heart reception

Once you self-identify as a creator and co-collaborator, manifestation from a heart focus becomes more straightforward. At heart you know what you desire to be, feel and do. Whereas the mind can be an ego dictator based in fear, lack and comparison, the heart is a loving director (or filter) of inspiration, optimism, and a multitude of blessings.

When we listen from the heart, we receive direct knowing of what serves the self and what benefits community. The shift from "I" to "We" is made. It's not that the individual no longer matters. It's that you have awakened to the truth that you can be your most authentic, brilliant self and serve something greater than convenience and consuming. It's that you can achieve for self and others at the same time. The sense of sharing one's radiance and one's life becomes more natural and integrated into the whole of humanity. This is the most basic meaning of multidimensional living.

Whether your community is focused on music and art, education and emotional health, nature and agriculture, animal protection and environmental conservation, political change and spirituality, the heart-centered benefits of taking part in community include:

* Living with clearer purpose

* Belonging in meaningful ways

* Enhanced sense of security

* Personal growth through group dynamics

* Development/improvement of leadership skills

* Learning to interact and collaborate effectively

* Receiving feedback on ideas and projects

* Authentic communication

* Playing with expansion of interests and abilities

* Living beyond personal desires by being of service

* Increased opportunities to be generous and gracious

* Balanced interaction (learning to give and receive)

* Potential for collective enlightenment

* More daily play

* Experience of group manifestation

* Practice of sacred rituals

* More reasons to celebrate

The heart is the best guide for any group or community that cares about making a difference and using this precious life to its fullest. Your heart will direct you and keep you on track. It just takes practice letting the heart lead, since most of us are so used to letting the head lead. As research from the Institute of HeartMath® has shown, heart focus creates significant shifts in perception, mental clarity and intuition. That's good news for intentional community.

Collective manifestation through community development makes each person an individual vehicle for manifestation and part of collective creation. It's the chance to live multi-dimensionally, to experience life as richer, more layered and fascinating. You get to explore how being your most brilliant self serves your life and others simultaneously.

Seven aspects of heart reception:

1. Heart reception is accessing the practical guidance and blueprints that come to your awareness and that resonate for your group.

2. Heart reception is tuning into intuitive guidance as a community or group. For instance, meditation, team creativity, story-telling, group discussions, intuitive processes, and specific tasks can facilitate information gathering from the heart.

3. Heart reception is what shows up through your collective strengths, gifts, talents and passions.

4. Heart reception is not about forcing anything to happen; it's about allowing, accepting, facilitating and being in flow. When you surrender having to control every aspect of your life, you expand your availability to the best possible outcomes.

5. Heart reception is a welcoming feeling. Such a tone actively encourages new ideas, projects, insights, and wonders to enter your consciousness and field of experience. We are connected to All That Is. Being in reception allows you to feel and welcome your divine connectedness.

6. Heart reception is an open attitude of expanded potential. Your life potential cannot be contained by the execution of mental goals and

dreams. Staying open to new inspiration, intuitive spontaneity, and synchronicity creates manifesting magic.

7. Heart reception is giving and receiving. You are the receiver and the sender of heart energy. It is not tit for tat. Generosity and gratitude simultaneously generate high-heart frequency. From a focus on what is good already, life feels magical and blessings will appear to propel you forward.

No matter how well-intentioned, trying to *make* things happen is old school. No more muscling outcomes into being. New paradigm manifesting energy is about sensing what can more easily show up through the container of conscious community. New community is about sacred heart *reception* that inspires intentional doing.

You are a receiver of wisdom, of inspiration, of ideas, of creativity, of motivation, of eagerness, of vision and of love energy in all its myriad forms. The wonderful thing about perceiving yourself as a receiver is that it creates an equal playing field amongst all group members. There's no expectation that one person is the holder of all the wisdom or know-how. Each person steps into their capabilities. This serves everyone: individual, group, and world.

For instance, my group focuses on receiving through a specific meditative visioning format that enables us to tune into our collective radar. Rather than driving a mental agenda or only receiving information individually, this format allows collective intuitive insights. The process enables us to receive new steps to take, and leaves room for unplanned growth and progress.

Yet, no matter the format you play with, it's important that heart-based vision, intention and compassion are the seeds you begin with. By practicing heart reception you open yourself up to a deeper understanding of what you and others might do with these seeds of creation.

Community offers many opportunities to learn lessons about what it means to both contribute and receive gifts through collaboration.

Your personal brilliance interacts, develops, and contributes to the progress of the group. Intentional community can advance humanity in ways far exceeding what any one person can achieve. It gives each of you a way to play bigger, be bolder, and to experience what it is to be part of a unified and energetic heart-force. When we are committed to empowering ourselves we empower our collective reality.

As Marianne Williamson states in *A Return to Love*, (and quoted by Nelson Mandela in his 1994 inaugural speech) "We are all meant to shine, as children do. We are born to make manifest the glory of God that is within us. It's not just in some of us, it's in everyone. And as we let our own light shine, we unconsciously give other people permission to do the same." Imagine if all communities on Earth gave their members permission to consciously shine? That's a domino effect worth embracing.

Chapter 3

Community Values

Pride makes us artificial
and humility makes us real
~ Thomas Merton, author and social critic

As you get into the process of creating new community, it feels important to acknowledge that *true home* is an inner residence. If you didn't learn it from Dorothy and her travels to Oz, then it's helpful to integrate this understanding now. It's a story that resonates because in our heart we know that we can never really leave home or get lost. On this life journey we carry our inner home with us wherever we are and it acts as our compass if we allow it to.

Consciously and unconsciously you are always creating your reality. The question is who are you putting in charge of your manifestation? Is your inner home run by the ego-mind or are you letting intuition (higher self, soul-essence) lead? The outer world manifests its shape and form via one's self-regard, personal perceptions, beliefs, choices, and reactions to unique life experiences. You cannot control the world. When you surrender to higher self, you create the intention to manifest beyond the limits of the ego-mind. Then you are able to step into the awesome power of the heart and soul.

To make the most significant changes in the world, it's critical to inhabit your whole self. As New Village 22 member Gabriele Neumann says, "Own your life, every inch and each corner of it."

If you have self-love for all your powerful masculine-feminine qualities, for all your balancing negative-positive aspects, you are more likely to thrive through the challenges of bringing vision into reality. If you have confidence and humility, as well as the ability to exert will and to surrender to outcome, you are truly poised to make a difference in the world. Fully owning your life is the conscious choice to lead life from the heart, rather than from the dictates of the mind. Clear signs that you're engaged at the heart level are:

* You feel enthusiasm and curiosity about what is currently unfolding in your life.

* You are inspired to focus your talents, skills and energy in a way that is more about creation and benefitting others than it is about ego satisfaction.

* When you don't know what to do in a challenging situation you surrender so that Infinite Grace can appear in surprising and often miraculous ways.

* Dissatisfaction with the status quo motivates you to make changes in your own thinking, doing and being.

* You sense that what your spiritual self has planned is way beyond the limited roles and so-called perks of "fitting in" and being socially accepted.

* Your intention is to be present for self and others.

New community is a heart and soul endeavor. Community co-creation is as simple as understanding that our inner homes are *already* connected energetically. So bringing new community into being is a natural extension of this energetic reality. Once our inner homes are in order, the manifestation of community more easily comes into being, and we can increasingly hold space for the appearance of heart-centered solutions to our greatest problems.

The longing for new community is a reminder that we are all in this together. If this beautiful planet is to continue being the wondrous life-giving physical home that it is, we all need to choose to coexist and create more harmoniously with it. When one person steps out of the dysfunctional patterns and habits of modern living that are "all take" and no "give back," the whole benefits.

As we collectively rebalance our inner selves — definitions of self-worth, beliefs about true capabilities, and approach to living one's life purpose — it follows that we imprint these changes on the outer world. Just as your body is an energy field, each new community is a field of energy. How unified this energy field is depends on the consistency with which agreed upon vision and priorities are integrated internally into your group's organizational and physical structures, and expressed outwardly through your relationships, services and creations.

Core values

A vital part of vision and focus is establishing clear core values that can be built into the fabric of your community. This creates an energetic center that radiates through all endeavors. By having core values everyone embraces and incorporates into everyday life, projects and products can more easily reflect and reinforce the values you deem vital.

For example, the core values for New Village 22 naturally flowed from conversations about what we would like to experience and our desire to hold energy for specific qualities of love, light and levity. You can have one core value or many more. What matters is your understanding of how these values are expressed through your community's presence and activities. No matter its size, your community has an energetic presence in the world. Core values help keep communication and contribution clear and on purpose. Our community is devoted to expressing and expanding the energy of:

1. Global Plenty. We believe there is enough for all. We support the plentiful, equitable and responsible sharing of personal gifts, knowledge and innovations, as well as earthly resources. All goodness and bounty radiates from the generous personal self that extends to munificent communities and to the world beyond.

2. Permission-based relationship with land, nature and earth. We ask the Spirit of Place what it requires and gives permission to. We make no presumptions about our relationships with land and the natural world. This is an area for the development of new respect and trust.

3. Love. We agree that community thrives and sustains itself on qualities of heart-connection and uplifted awareness. Compassion and understanding are integral. Our communal heart establishes a signature energetic presence.

4. Full, Fun Engagement. We are committed to bringing our best selves to our participation. We're all in! We do not hold back, as we're not tied to social norms or to other's opinions of us. This big "Yes" to the Universe is a playful approach to fulfilling collective brilliance. We'll take "wild and weird" over "same-old" any day. We do not take ourselves too seriously and we believe in having fun.

5. Discovery. Wonder, curiosity, exploration, experimentation, and innovation are qualities of an unlimited path of discovery. We see ourselves as pioneers of possibility.

6. Non-judgmental Creativity. We are creative beings at play — dreaming, imagining, intuiting, and experimenting. We integrate and cross-weave diverse disciplines without bias. We create to experience universal potential, without fear of judgment. We create as expressions of love and light.

7. Female-Male Equality. Each individual is an aspect of All That Is, a free being of universal light. No single light source has more natural authority than another. We possess qualities that are both masculine and feminine and wish to bring a balance of these to our manifestation.

8. Non-hierarchical Collaboration, Cooperation, and Exchange. We aspire to freely bring our individual brilliance into form and expression for the good of all. We stay flexible as to what opportunities show up and how we can best participate. We learn to thrive in a collaborative atmosphere in which everyone communicates authentically and is seen, heard, and valued.

9. Change. Our community is a change-maker through an inward-to-outward process. Focused change is highly desirable. Surprising change is accepted. Change is the flexible operating system by which we create at a high level. Change spurs growth, while inhibiting stagnation and entropy. Transformation occurs as we delve into the unknown and let divine wisdom lead the process.

10. Global Connection. We come together remotely from across the globe, and we recognize our connection to all. We actively connect internationally to access wisdom and learning, and welcome participation from people of all parts of the world.

**Collective Manifestation Blueprint Exercise:
Core Values**

1. List values that are important to you or that are currently resonating with you. You can combine values in any way you chose. You

might consider creating statements that clarify how the value will be expressed in your community. Here is a list of values to consider:

Abundance	Contribution	Fun	Order
Ethical living	Safety	Generosity	Conservation
Health	Courage	Growth	Passion
Achievement	Grace	Awe	Peace
Adventure	Creativity	Honesty/ Integrity	Self development
Fairness challenge	Curiosity	Impeccability	Physical
Authenticity	Decisiveness	Independence	Accountability
Authority	Purity	Awareness	Pleasure
Influence	Diversity	Inner peace	Love of animals
Happiness	Privacy	Recreation	Empowerment
Leisure	Economic security	Intuition	Balance
Beauty	Productivity	Joy	Public service
Caring	Efficiency	Change	Delight
Challenge	Serenity	Knowledge	Quality relationships
Justice	Excellence	Leadership	Intellect
Clarity	Ecological stewardship	Cooperation	Respect self/ others
Co-creation	Experience	Excitement	Discovery
Spirituality	Humor	Love	Flow/Ease
Truth	Family	Connection	Learning
Competence	Activism	Meaningful work	Ethical practice
Flexibility	Freedom	Love of nature	Service
Confidence	Self-Esteem	Momentum	Gratitude
Loyalty	Friendship	Well-being	Openness
Unity	Focus	Sustainability	Support
Stability	Compassion	Plenty	Wisdom
Wonder	Simplicity	Mindfulness	Solitude/Quiet

2. Ask yourself or your group the following questions about the values you have selected:

   * Why does the particular value matter in the development of your community?

   * How does each value reinforce the vision you hold for community?

   * How does that value add to the creation of a better world and universe?

3. Discuss/decide how you will communicate your values to new members.

Collective Manifestation Blueprint Exercise:
Community Wishes

Have a discussion about members' wishes for your community and all of humanity. Make this a heart-based discussion. You know when you've hit on a heart wish because you'll feel easy exuberance. To get you started here are some sample wishes:

   * Peace.

   * Excitement about what each person contributes.

   * Cooperation and unified strength.

   * Joyful play.

   * Learning that flows easily.

* Physical structures that support bringing the impossible into possibility.

* Best use of energies.

* Broadcasting solutions to the greater world-universe.

* Holding high frequency in quirky and magical ways.

* Facilitating knowing, inventions, and discovery.

* Transformation through creativity.

2. List your wishes. They can relate to the overall atmosphere you would like to create, the physical structures you would like to build, the energy you would like to generate, and the outcomes of that. List here or in your journal:

1.

2.

3.

4.

5.

Chapter 4

Pillars of Focus

When people see more clearly,
they act more clearly and powerfully.
~ Steve Davis, FacilitatorU.com founder

I n 2012, I had a dream with the clear and pressing message: "Connect the islands of light!" Intuitively this felt like a message about uniting with others to radiate the energy of love, light and levity throughout the world.

I love the vision of intentional communities (already in existence and those being formed at this very moment) as connected islands or oases of light that bring all of humanity into a cohesive and healed whole. Although it's the most audacious vision I've ever received, it also feels very doable. As Ted Andrews wrote in his seminal work, *Animal Speak*, "The bee reminds us that no matter how great the dream, there is the promise of fulfillment if we pursue it."

Collective manifestation shift: From followers to initiators

With each remarkable person I spoke with for this book, I began to see that this connection of light was already happening. Fresh waves of potential are indeed circulating around the globe in surprising ways.

You are each a creator, a radiant presence designed to shine. You are being asked to own your brilliance for the benefit of all.

Artist Darrell Toland showed great initiative and creative passion by installing a nearly 12-foot tall robot sculpture in the front yard of his home. Often art installations are relegated to corporate parks and city squares. By following his heart with this residential installation, Darrell has created a new neighborhood "connector." Children marvel at it, leaving gifts of rock and flowers in the welcoming outstretched hand of the friendly robot with the heart that lights up. Adults slow down as they drive past. Pedestrians stop to chat about the surprising yard adornment. Darrell says about the artwork's ripple effect, "It's definitely changed the energy on the street in a good way. Yesterday, I overheard someone on their phone giving directions. They said 'Turn left at the robot. Don't worry what robot, you'll know.'"

This story hints at the potential for expanded creativity to add a dimension to our communities we didn't even know was missing. It shows how following one's passions is a magnet that attracts others by its very audaciousness. When you express from the heart you give permission to others to express more boldly and more authentically. Subsequently, we have a culture that is more heart-centered, inclusive, and naturally promotes a higher degree of creativity.

> *You are the river of humanity that will simply flow around the current societal obstructions toward evolution, healing, and advancement for self, others and all living beings.*

People are increasingly being attracted to others who share their vision and heart-centered goals. We are coming together instinctively as a brilliant network of inspired and lit up co-initiators who are charged up with renewed energy and purpose. The dream of all kinds of communities full of truly connected, devoted, and engaged individuals is real. You and your community members will continue to, or begin to, link up your brilliance in powerful, fun and significant ways that will newly shape every aspect of society for the better. You are the architects of heaven on earth. By connecting, we affirm that the immense potential we sense building up is real.

In addition, cross-pollination and exciting interaction among these communities of co-initiators will influence more traditional communities and create the possibility for an even greater cumulative positive planetary effect. The islands of light that are meant to unite will do so I am sure.

Collective Manifestation Blueprint Exercise: Centralize Your Brilliance

1. If you have not done so already, keep a folder of ideas and inspiration that you notice. This may relate to architectural and sustainable design, environmental innovations, articles about interesting property/building rehabilitations, tips about effective group organization, stories about what other focused groups are creating, and so forth. This can be an online folder. You will be inspired by what you find already taking shape on this precious planet.

2. If you are prone to drawing and doodling, as I am, then dedicate a notebook or sketch pad to drawings related to your community project. This will help put energy behind what resonates for you, and to give form to your ideas, insights, and intentions.

Pillars of focus

One way to consciously build a network of helpful connections is to create focus that attracts particular people and ideas to your projects and the spirit of your community. In my case, once the founding members of New Village 22 had been invited to join me and our core values identified, agreeing on the central focus for our community was pretty straightforward. We each have specific areas of expertise that we are jointly interested in exploring, and that are already integral to our idea of living a satisfying and joyful life.

The pillars of focus for New Village 22 are creativity, learning and energy. These were chosen as a match for our primary interests and gifts, and they will help us bring cohesive purpose to the projects we develop. These pillars will help us attract additional members who are stimulated by such focus. Our three pillars of focus are:

1. **Creativity Pillar** — Our aim is to be creative at each point of New Village 22's development. From the start, we agreed we did not need to work with existing templates for creation. We certainly had no desire to push out plans simply from the brain. Rather our aim is to create from a multidimensional understanding of the universe and our place in it. It is our hope that this creative umbrella will awaken and accelerate playful paths of exploration, discovery and implementation, as well as stimulate radiant play in all the creative arts from painting and music to performance and carpentry. We create in an atmosphere of curiosity and openness. We strive to notice new ways to complement one another's interests and projects. What is created and experienced in one area can easily inform and pollinate another area. Quite simply, more creativity equals more possibility at play.

2. **Learning Pillar** — We begin with the understanding that life is learning. We embrace our teacher/student selves and look for the lessons in even the most challenging life situations. We agree that we can never know it all, and love creating new opportunities for learning. We learn from each other — listening to each other's stories and making inquiries that draw out new insights and access points for learning. We believe that learning occurs multi-dimensionally: mentally, emotionally, physically and spiritually. This learning focus will

naturally include projects around education development. For example, how it can work more effectively and benefit people of all ages, and how technology will continue to shape educational possibilities, and connect us to teachers from around the world. This learning focus is non-traditional, non-linear and is fueled by interest and curiosity rather than led by teaching agendas.

3. **Energy Pillar** — This is an essential focus. We began the creation of New Village 22 by playing in the invisible energy field by initiating a meditative visioning process. The idea is that by beginning here, we bring greater consciousness to that which is manifested. (You will read more about this process in Part Two.) We acknowledge that all is energy. We believe in energy healing for humans and the ability to heal and work with the energy of place and space. We aspire to the creation of more sustainable ways to live, as well as to energy-efficient/energy-generating innovative design. We integrate geomancy, feng shui, numerology, astrology and so forth in our consideration of what influences energy, and facilitates working with energy. We believe in cosmic energy and the ability to perceive helpful energy from spiritual guides and sources.

With these three pillars of focus in place we easily direct our heart-centered energy, focus our impulses for discovery and learning, and expand our collaborative energy.

Collective Manifestation Blueprint Exercise:
What Are Your Community Pillars of Focus?

Community can rarely be all things to all people. The truth is that a community works best through intentional creation. I've read accounts about "unintentional" communities created back in the sixties. For a while these communities were non-conventional places for experimentation, achievement, adventure and fun. Without clear focus though, they tended to fall apart or become something else entirely. Without focus it is also difficult to take what is developed out to the greater community. Community without centering focus is likely to become more like an isolated bubble, and that does not serve the greater good effectively.

1. Review the following questions as you define the central focuses of your community:

    *   What natural areas of expertise do your members have?

    *   What new areas of investigation would you like to foster?

    *   What projects does the world need the most help with?

    *   What areas of interest do your founding members have the most passion around?

    *   As an individual, what types of communities might you be interested in connecting to?

    *   What concepts-themes-innovations are on the horizon? Are you interested in being part of or leading this energy wave?

    *   What have you always thought would be really cool, if it were possible to create?

    *   What's your vision for everyday life in your community? What opportunities are present?

    *   What social issues or hot buttons are currently getting your attention?

    *   Do you know of any causes or organizations your community may align with or support?

2. Based on your responses, list central and emerging areas for focus:

1.

2.

3.

—⁕—

Individual and coherent community needs

It's great to be visionary, but you also have physical, emotional and mental needs. Acknowledging these needs contributes to your sense of wholeness and generates a clearer vision that contributes to living life full out.

To ensure that we understood the needs of our members we each completed a survey. From that our members expressed the following needs:

* To create

* To celebrate

* To be inspired

* To encourage others

* To be part of a greater purpose

* To experience beauty

* To be joyful

* To retreat

* To have flexibility

* To foster organic organization

To create and to celebrate were at the top of our list. A powerful "needs" combination — for creation is a kind of celebration of life, and what is co-creation without the ritual of celebration that affirms what is developed and comes to light? As Paula stated, "I think celebration creates community and is a very deep form of communal prayer."

She also beautifully described flexibility this way: "Flexibility means space for each individual within the community and being gentle with the mind/body/heart of each person. It means creating a framework for organizing life in the village and bending when and wherever necessary without losing focus."

Gabriele felt that the needs of inspiration, beauty and joy were the "closest to an angelic feeling." For her the needs process was about identifying the essence of an ideal state of being that she would love to experience on a daily basis.

For myself, I experience creation and celebration as essential to fully-engaged living and feeling blessed. As an introvert, it is also vital to me that individuals have independence and quiet time for reflection and recharging. As you may recall, the original idea that gave birth to this community project was the dream to create a retreat center. So I bring this need for spiritual and energetic refreshment forward to New Village 22.

Encouraging others, fostering organic organization, and being part of a greater purpose naturally align to our desire to create, learn and energize in such a way that the benefits spiral ever outward beyond the core of our small community.

By naming these needs we lay the foundation for each community member to experience a meaningful life full of creativity, joy and inspired beauty. We connect in cooperation, encouragement and celebration as we recognize the presence of sacred purpose.

Collective Manifestation Blueprint Exercise:
Community Member Needs (individual and collective)

One key to grounding your community in reality is making it an expression of real needs. By identifying the needs of your members, your intention is to set the tone on behalf of all of those who will eventually join your endeavor. Of course, needs evolve over time, so this is a valuable "checking-in" process that can be used at various points in your community evolution. Have each member complete the following:

1. Indicate your top 3 needs (that you envision being incorporated into your community dynamic)

To appreciate	To learn	To grow	To be inspired
To belong	To be welcomed	To be engaged	To have greater purpose
To be surprised	To discover	To be accessible	To bring community together
To be comfortable	To be safe	To play	To have structure
To be artistic	To be heard	To have a voice	To contribute
To have retreat	To rejuvenate soul	To live sustainably	To lead
To create	To celebrate	To be recognized	To experience beauty
To experiment	To be supported	To have peace	To encourage others
To be healed	To blossom	To have choice	To experience diversity
To have flexibility	To share	To experience magic	To have sensory experience
To be fulfilled	To leave a legacy	To be authentic	To raise vibration

To have intimate relationships	To break free from the status quo	To foster organic organization	To share life experience
To bring about new social systems	To protect and care for the natural world	To be part of an interesting eco-system	To live multi-dimensionally

Other:

Please explain or define the needs you selected in more detail:

Chapter 5

Release and Healing Into Oneness

I am the daughter of Earth and Water,
And nursling of the Sky...I change, but I cannot die.
~ Percy Bysshe Shelley, English romantic poet

We are experiencing what happens when the head (mental logic) rules the world. We end up stressed out, over worked, over stimulated, and trying to reward ourselves with a mountain of stuff. The ego-mind, based in fear and lack, sets up a competitive field in which "might makes right" and "the end justifies the means."

The collective awakening occurring for humanity has presented us with opportunities to clear wounds of the past, old stories of victimhood, and outdated paradigms that repress rather than liberate wholeness of spirit.

This inner house clearing has been necessary to make energetic space for new, evolving possibilities that want to show up. Space clearing includes recognizing disempowering habits of thought and doing, and releasing energy-sapping relationships that no longer nourish the soul. Individuals who do the deep work of recognizing the resistance to change that lies within themselves, can then better empower any group effort to change the world.

Individually, you can create this space by releasing old stories about what you are capable of doing and being. You create space by letting go of old alignments that no longer serve you. You create spaciousness by integrating the various aspects of your whole self — aspects that you may have disowned or ignored before now. You create space through stillness. You make this space by setting ego-mind demands aside and putting soul in the driver's seat of your community vision. If you have organized and expanded your sense of inner home, you can more easily envision how outer reality might mirror it.

Author Joyce Anderson's passion for creating community comes from the hurt of having a child that doesn't fit in. As she says, "I was putting my hurt onto my son. Wanting him to be fixed was really a sign that I needed to fix myself." She took this recognition and put it into form. First, into a book about how we bury our gifts through comparison, and recently she launched a "Silent Parenting" program that helps parents of kids with learning differences work on releasing their worries and developing patience. According to Joyce, it's a fundamental shift from an outer focus to an inner focus. "It's not about what you do as a parent; it's about who you are."

Holding space for what wants to flow through you is an ongoing process of releasing what is no longer needed or helpful. History, wounds of humanity, and Earth trauma is reflected in the landscape around us. As we continue to clear trauma, and heal fractures of spirit, personally and collectively, we become more aware of what we willingly leave behind in order to create space for what we hope to bring forward and manifest into being.

In our community process, we came to key points in which intentional personal clearing and healing felt like a natural and necessary step for the intentional expansion of collective consciousness. By healing personal aspects like family issues, we perceived that we created "new branches" or "arteries" for information and wisdom to travel to the collective mind.

Collective manifestation shift:
From fearful control to trusting grace

What needs to be released collectively continues to be a fascinating journey. During what has been called the shift of consciousness on this planet over the last several years, a few key aspects of societal programming have begun to be released, consciously and unconsciously, by much of humankind. Namely, we are releasing:

* Patriarchal control (a fabulous book about this is *Unplugging the Patriarchy* by Lucia Rene). This is release of the need to be told what to do and owning your inner authority and guidance.

* Mindless, trance-like adherence to consumer-based value systems that bring wealth to a few and impoverish many.

* Ego-mind leadership based on competition, comparison, and control. This is the release of hierarchy in favor of heart-based cooperation, collaboration and mutual regard.

* Growth-stifling attachment to personal agendas based in fear

A symptom of this shift is the fierce opposition and resistance to change by factions clinging to the old paradigm. It's the death throes of mental, patriarchal, material, fear-based systems. Despite the chaos of system changes, we all know when we need to release and to clear. Our language tells us when "we've had it up to here," and "we can't take any more." We see this at the personal level, and in the world, in all the ways that we leak our brilliance rather than direct it effectively. This is a call to pause, evaluate and discern what is outdated and limiting, and recognize that our personal choices are creating our collective future.

During this initial stage of my own community development, I was flooded by intense energy from my brother who was enmeshed in a dramatic life scenario — one that his fearful ego-mind created, clinging to the need to experience itself as a victim. Anger, blame, frustration with circumstances, inertia, and the desire to have someone swoop in and save him played out in many variations. I knew this was a small-scale dynamic playing out across the planet.

When new energy waves from his troubles appeared, I was reminded in meditation to keep "washing it through, washing it through" so I didn't hold onto energy that would overwhelm me, and that wasn't mine to begin with. I learned vital lessons around surrender at this time — part of the gifts my brother's chaotic situation presented. I realized that only by surrendering my own ego-mind fears about his situation could I hold open-heart space for grace to appear in unimaginable ways. And it did, time and time again. I had the opportunity to release generations of familial co-dependency by expressing love and compassion, and by offering appropriate support without forcing a fix that he would have probably rejected anyway. None of us can control others or the situations they create. We can only choose to hold light for the best possible outcome for all, whatever that proves to be.

As this situation taught me, it's appropriate that such intense personal learning be applied to intentional community building. You are invited to end your connection to unnecessary drama and mental attachments so that you have energetic and physical room in your life for what really matters. You are invited to end mindless societal programming so that you can show up as your true empowered self. What this makes room for in the collective energy field is:

* Integration of the divine masculine and feminine so that humanity is able to be more balanced in the presentation of the mental, physical and spiritual gifts being offered to the world.

* Opportunities to mature as we learn to skillfully ride the waves of tension created by holding opposite viewpoints with more equilibrium.

* Formation of new love currencies, vital to connected energy based on trust, good faith and equitable exchange.

* Spirit-led leadership — that is authentic and grounded, inspiring and inclusive, generous and fair, a reflection of one's most visionary and magnanimous self.

* Collective vision as a sum total of individual missions that are beautifully woven together for fascinating, innovative and effective outcomes.

Individually this expansion of consciousness demonstrates itself in various ways. It can show up as a new urge toward activism (taking back your power in some manner on behalf of the planet and the collective), or as a fresh service-based career path. For me it appeared as a desire to toss out all my old photo albums since I intuited that I was no longer that person. If I was to truly end a mindset of comparison and competition, than I needed to stop comparing my present self to an old version of myself (especially since my old self played by societal rules and the new me is playing in an unlimited field of multidimensional experience). It's the chance to expand a personal dream into a dream for all.

Collective Manifestation Blueprint Exercise:
Identifying What to Release and Clear

Over a 24-hour period note when you feel limited, stuck, self-berating, distracted and disengaged. Then consider and answer the following questions:

* What are you aware of that you wish to release and clear (co-dependency, specific fears or phobias, habits of distraction, limiting beliefs, etc.)?

* What will this make room for in your life?

* What outdated desires would you like to release (the desire for scads of possessions, an old dream that has been replaced by a better vision, the need to retire, etc.)?

* What does your community group wish to release and clear on behalf of the empowerment of humanity?

Collective Manifestation Blueprint Exercise:
Releasing — A Guided Meditation

Realizing what is holding you back from your true potential — guilt, worry, or feeling undeserving — is the first step. Yet, even once identified you may be at a loss as to how to process this knowledge and how to truly release yourself from the old programming. You may regularly think things like: "I feel guilty that my sibling has such a hard life," or "I can't release worry, it is part of how I operate in the world," or "For as long as I can remember I have feared getting my Dad's genes." Try the following guided meditation as a regular part of clearing and release.

1. Gather your group for a releasing session, or agree to each do this individually.

2. Sit comfortably and take a couple cleansing breaths and close your eyes.

3. *Imagine that you are holding a dandelion in front of your face. Each seed filament represents all that may be released for your highest good. You might recall how you blew the seedy tops of dandelions as a child, scattering the many seeds and floating away on a breeze.*

Imagine that each dandelion seed is a worry, a specific guilt, a belief that holds you back from true expansion. Like the dandelion you need to let go of all these aspects in order to expand your energetic presence in the world. This is a time to release tension, and any fear-based contractions so that you can go with the flow.

Blow on the round seed head of your imaginary dandelion. Blow a number of times (whatever feels right or necessary). Send the seeds floating off into the wind. They disperse and flutter like little helicopters. What feels like a weed in your life is actually a growth generator.

Keep blowing into your dandelion. Some filaments may be tenacious. Blow firmly with the sure force of your clear will — your willingness to release these personality aspects.

You blow and release the energy of worry, guilt, fear, unworthiness, lack of confidence. As you blow, feel joy in your heart. Smile knowing that they will seed new growth elsewhere.

Thank the guilt, the worry, the self-judgment that clung to you. For the presence of these aspects have given you a gift that you can now release. You can now discern how it helped you grow. You can thank it for serving its purpose.

Feel your expansion. Feel your openness. You are now a receptor for the opposite of these qualities. Repeat to yourself: I am (we are) a receptor for calm, kindness, courage, self-love and confidence. Name the qualities you mindfully wish to embody.

When this visualization feels complete, thank the dandelion. Thank the weeds that nurture your growth. Feel the humor and perfection in this — that weeds are seeds. Close this exercise by repeating "Amen,

Amen, Amen" or any other words that create closure for you (Fini, True, Let it be, etc.).

Repeat this exercise any time you become aware of worry, guilt, fear, and "not-good-enough" thoughts or mental tracks that you would like to release.

Alternate exercise #1:
1. Write what you wish to release on separate pieces of paper.

2. With a heart full of love put these pieces of paper in a fire. Release each one, voicing what it is you release and what alchemy will arise from the ashes of this release, such as "I release co-dependency, so that I can master self-empowerment." Release with love. Trust that the energy of love can transmute these challenges appropriately.

Alternative exercise #2:
Jena Griffiths, who is the founder of Earth School, an online forum where healers and authors share their wisdom, also believes we heal the planet when we heal ourselves. She recommends the simple Hawaiian practice of Ho'oponopono to release limiting thoughts.

1. "Whenever you have a limiting thought about yourself of any kind simply apologize to yourself for having the thought. You can say, 'I'm sorry. Please forgive me. Thank you. I love you.' Or just one of these sentences, if you prefer. That's all there is to it. You'll be amazed."

Individual growth equals group growth
It's important to realize that each member of your community will continue to process personal issues that present growth opportunities

for themselves and for the group. Working as a team inevitably makes this concept very real. As Gabriele so eloquently stated:

Energetically working together means the energy will be much stronger than if one was processing alone. You invite grander forces to carry and support you. Every issue that comes up for the project has an impact on the team members, and what comes up for each individual has an impact on the project. As each person clears personal blockages and issues, the team more and more learns how to clear the way for the project to unfold and 'upgrade its light' in the world.

Authentic community process requires awareness that personal and group growth is a dynamic that will be quite visible. If people are relating authentically, the focus won't be about how to look good, fit in, and say the right things. Exchanges will be about showing up as your best self in the moment. Not perfect, just honestly engaged. That's enough.

Often our familial, cultural and societal programming makes authenticity a challenge. I've encountered people who say they are intuitive and awake, and yet their behavior indicates they are still in hiding — afraid to be fully seen lest others find them too "woo-woo" or even cuckoo. This actually causes intuition to shut down and inhibits strong connections to others. If you're afraid of what others think of you, then you are going in and out of authenticity. Intuitive astrologer Sarah Varcas says that through discernment we can live more authentically.

Within this process of discernment we encounter the challenge to look directly and without guile at our lives, not seeking to blame or excuse ourselves or anyone else, not trying to side-step the areas of which we are less proud or about which we experience shame, but instead just looking with open eyes and a heart to match, in order to see clearly the adjustment necessary at this time. The challenge is to make our actions match the truth of ourselves and our situation. It is time to stop beating ourselves over the head with old beliefs about who we should be and instead embrace who we are and the full flowering of our true potential, whatever form it takes. We only have to be ourselves as fully as possible, in order to contribute our own unique resonance to the collective energy field.

Be gentle with yourself. It's a process of releasing the inauthentic layers so that you fully inhabit your shiny self, no matter how quirky or different. This kind of authenticity, freedom and personal empowerment might not feel natural, and it doesn't always make others comfortable, because you mirror new potential for others to own. Whether or not they are ready to embrace it is not up to you.

Raja Choudhury, who started the "Spirituality and Consciousness" community on LinkedIn five years ago, said that when a discussion group heckler shows up, they are treated with love. "When someone starts ranting, and no one knows what they are talking about, ten people will say, 'I love you, I feel your pain,' and POOF the negative person disappears."

As a leader and active participant, the changes you are making in society and the business world will trigger fear in others who will insist "that's not how it's done" or "that's not reality." Megan Gaiser, a leader who is passionate about bringing change to the gaming industry, has run into such fear responses and has found that meeting fear resistance with heart is a powerful way to turn naysayers into supporters. As she says, "Staying present, listening with openness, compassion and curiosity, positively changes the dynamic."

The most effective groups will be comprised of people who don't mind engaging and supporting opportunities for personal growth and collective growth because they understand it is the foundation of new community and world evolution. It's about inhabiting a new personal pattern of "being out of the ordinary" so that communities can be extraordinary.

Barbara Krauss, creativity coach and the fourth member of New Village 22 (who joined a year into our process), believes in the value of working in groups. "We experience how to foster a deeper understanding of each other and our collective purpose, which is a critical component for creating meaningful lives, responsible citizenship, and an empowered sense of self in an interdependent world."

Beneficial community dynamics

I am sensing in others an eagerness to jump into community and group building. The creative impulse to address global issues, to make daily living more of an adventure, and to relate at a deeper level with others abounds.

Personally, I love learning as I go along, yet there is so much wisdom available from people and groups who have already been engaged in community building. Suzanne Anderson has participated in and helped to form many different types of community. For many years she lived in a spiritual community in Canada. Eventually the hierarchy of the old community paradigm was a serious detriment to both satisfying daily community participation and to sustaining community over the long haul, even within the context of a shared spiritual focus. "I was part of a wave in changing this. I loved the sense of belonging and liked participating, but I rebelled against the roles." So her participation was not predicated on going along with the status quo. When she experienced inequality, she worked within the group structure to effect change.

Eventually Suzanne would leave this spiritual community and live in a communal home in Toronto. This enabled her to go off into the world and work, while still having a loving environment full of friendship to come home to each night. Her love of community would also lead her to live on a small island in Washington State. This small community living was a different manifestation of community, and satisfying in its own way. Suzanne recognizes that community is a dominant thread that runs through her life and she is currently feeling into how it will manifest next.

Kris Steinnes founded Women of Wisdom in 1993 as an event-driven community of women dedicated to honoring the feminine spirit and the contribution of women to society. This gives her great insight into what does and doesn't work within the context of a true shared community.

According to Kris, the form that facilitates active group participation is the circle. "The circle dynamic is ancient, but it eliminates hierarchy and allows everyone to be heard and respected for what they value. It creates bonding and respect. It allows the quiet voices to be heard."

This dynamic that Women of Wisdom practices as a collective core value comes from Christina Baldwin's *The Circle Way*. The circle principle includes sharing of responsibilities, rotating leadership, bringing your gifts, being present, contributing, and putting spirit (who you are) in the center of the circle. Kris believes that the circle is a safe container for sharing and makes it easy to refocus on a group's central purpose. "We hide because we don't want to be wrong and stand out differently. We want to be accepted and loved. Yet, if you're sitting back and not contributing you're not fully engaging and being part of community. The practice of circle sharing and getting support allows you to step out of limits and puts a leader in every seat."

The Women of Wisdom community uses communication tools to facilitate circle dynamics. Kris says that tools that honor individuals and the group include asking collaborative-buy-in questions like "How does everyone else feel?" and healing circles that facilitate conflict resolution. Kris explains, "A healing circle model allows for all voices to come forward in conflict situations and to co-create solutions as a group, including the need for new policies and procedures. That's community."

Collective Manifestation Blueprint Exercise: Organizational Processes

1. Consider processes that will facilitate your particular group's interaction and problem solving.

2. If appropriate, research processes used by other groups and communities. Areas for research might include:

* Dynamics of collaboration and co-operation.

* Facilitation of out-of-the-box creativity.

* How to encourage member cohesiveness and participation.

* Principals of effective communication.

* Conflict resolution.

* Feedback processes.

3. Agree upon and implement foundational processes. Make sure that each community co-creator is comfortable with the tools and processes you will be asking them to use and take part in. This is a fun learning and exchange opportunity.

Chapter 6

The Power of Play

*"Let's help each other create a better world
through play, laughter and creativity."*
~ Mary Alice Long, psychotherapist and writer

A wareness is play. It's also a foundational change tool that can complement nearly any process for community development and discovery, whether you jump right in with active initiatives or proceed more slowly. The practice of awareness in daily life will put you on a playful manifesting path, unlike a mental approach that works hard and muscles through to find answers. All is in front of you; all you need do is trust in your ability to access it.

The world is full of distraction from your true powers. Awareness allows you to sense what exists to be seen, heard, touched, and known. Some awareness basics:

✱ Be observant and discuss with your co-creators what you are noticing coming into your field of awareness. I keep a separate document where I retain all the points of interest I come across (in articles, books, photos, films, and so forth).

* Notice what is being shared in social media that catches your attention.

* Discover what innovators are discussing; discover what philanthropists are doing.

* Notice synchronicities. What might those synchronicities lead you to investigate?

* Follow the people connections that appear in your life. Consider whether you have something to learn from a new connection or how they may contribute to your community.

Pieces of information, snippets of conversation, and resources from friends are bread crumbs that the Universe leaves for you to find. It's up to you to connect the dots. What you gather through awareness will eventually make sense and link to other puzzle pieces.

Collective Manifestation Blueprint Exercise:
Playfully Energizing Your Community
Discuss the following questions with your community members or potential members.

* What kind of community are you? List descriptive words and phrases like: cloistered, open, multi-generational, mid-life focused, family-oriented, non-hierarchical, research-based, arty, activist, physical, nurturing, educational, service-oriented, agricultural, mystical, divine feminine, and so forth.

* What do you intend to create/innovate/process/grow/broadcast/provide or give form to on behalf of the greater community of humankind?

✳ If your community was an adventure/amusement/land (or location/place) what would it be called?

✳ Who do you want to attract to participate in your community?

✳ What is the boldest, most audacious, radical or playful thing you can imagine your community doing-instigating-creating-offering-becoming?

✳ What other communities would you like to align with? For instance, we hope to align with healing and agricultural communities.

—✄—

Just as forcing things to happen is passé, the old process of creation as hard work is outdated. No more exhausting yourself and stressing yourself out for some perceived life improvement that doesn't actually add quality to your life or to the lives of others.

No longer do we have to try to squeeze life satisfaction out of rationed "advertising" events and holidays. Through a heart-centered approach to life we can choose to appreciate and love all of life. The companies that try to sell us things we don't need for life satisfaction won't like this. Yet, it's an empowering shift that *is* happening.

Collective manifestation shift:
From hard work to inspired play

It's time to shift from a mindset of work to a mindset of play. This naturally shifts us from an end-result focus to an in-the-moment focus. Play is an important aspect of our current manifesting abilities.

Play is both a mindset and a way to facilitate group interaction. New intentional community is about joining together to create places and ways for our physical bodies, emotions, imaginations and spiritual consciousness to play. Collective manifestation is about making a difference through purposeful and playful engagement of your gifts, talents and personalities. Effectiveness and humor can align. It's about joyfully persevering and inspiring others to lighten up and have more fun. Playing with our sacred oneness enables spirit to show up in amazing fashions.

Play aligns with the natural rhythms of life. By establishing a loving and inspired playground for co-creation, you collectively have a wonderful opportunity to practice being unlimited vehicles for light and for anchoring in new possibilities that are equal parts fun and fanciful, useful and serious.

Mary Alice Long is a play-based depth-oriented psychotherapist, coach, speaker-performer, and trainer. Play is the specialty she brings to both her business, Play = Peace, and residential community. It's her mission to create a life that comes from the heart through play. As she says, "Play is engaging, play is life giving, play is whimsical, play is profound."

Mary Alice believes that play is our birthright at every age. "Even though we are socialized out of play at an early age through our schooling, and even though play and imagination have been ripped out of the typical adult life, our unconscious invites us to play in both our sleeping and waking worlds. We can take an attitude of play no matter what we doing and this brings more joy, ease and health into our lives, our relationships and our projects. Incorporating play into any strategy naturally makes people more effective and collaborative."

There are many benefits to taking a playful approach to life and community participation. Mary Alice points out that "play creates a more conscious and effective mind-body connection. Play can bring more balanced energy to leadership styles and group dynamics." Play as it turns out can help with issues as diverse as organizational problems and processing grief.

One tip that Mary Alice offers for getting into the spirit of play is to begin in your imagination. "Even if you don't feel like being outright playful, you can play with imagination and it has all the same benefits." Every part of your mind that is engaged when you play outright is engaged by imaging play. It's like imaginary recess.

As I spoke with people about building community, the theme of fostering fun and inspiration came up from people of all walks of life and with very different work focuses. This shift into a play mindset is a vital aspect of community — from creating authentic connections and re-imagining the education system to creating sustainable lifestyles and bringing about social change. As Long related, "Getting good grades, doing the expected things, those were things I did for my parents. When I reclaimed play in my life, my life became so different, so amazing. Options opened up. I see all the choices. I can go with my passion."

Play is a perfect way to act on inspirations. Massage therapist and wellness educator Heidi Frank, and educator and AD/HD coach Margit Crane started a series of free hug events in order to be catalysts for community connection. Each had their own impetus for manifesting this event. Heidi explains, "I'm a hugger by heart. These events are a social experiment to see what kind of comfortable space I can provide for others by letting myself be vulnerable first. I was floating by the end of our first hug event." Margit says her intent is to share love without needing to know exactly how it helps each person. "When I'm hugging people, I'm healing them. So many people don't know what to ask for, or what healing they need. This is my way of making others feel better so that they are inspired to share more love." For both women, the events have nothing to do with running an agenda and everything to do with co-creating in the moment with others.

Community environments can be physically shaped through play. Adam White is an award-winning landscape architect and co-director of Davies White Landscape Architects based in England. He applies his love of watching things grow, engagement and play to create remarkable playscapes that thrill kids and adults alike. It's his way of contributing to the quality of community living, and to bringing nature into urban spaces. "We're a small group of landscape architects that want to change a little bit of the world for communities to enjoy. We need more of our open spaces to be fun, like quirky seating and swings at bus stops." Adam's latest project, the Dinton Pastures Country Park in Wokingham Borough, England, features nest towers, swing hanging logs, zip wires, troll holes, climbing logs, a play bridge, a willow maze, a story-telling area and a woodland obstacle course. "Our innovatively designed wild design rejects preconceived notions of a playground in favor of a more natural approach to play," he states about the firm's desire to encourage engagement with the natural surroundings and kids being able to take acceptable levels of risk that create excitement. To Adam the whole environment should have play value.

Kids and adults alike can play their way toward positive outcomes. This includes playing with how you receive knowledge and knowing, how you educate yourself and fuel personal growth, how you exercise and use your creativity. Play is a great attitude to take as you explore the many ways that you can be, think, feel, and act. Play amplifies energy into expressions of higher, deeper, wider, and louder. It encourages boldness and adventure. There are many paths to a successful life. More and more we are waking up to the fact that the process of getting to our goals can be enjoyable, exhilarating and easier if we take an attitude of play.

Collective Manifestation Blueprint Exercise: Incorporating Play

1. For many adults play needs to be practiced before it integrates as a natural part of life. Consider the following questions to determine how you can be more playful.

    * How could your talents and gifts be expressed in a more playful manner?

    * How could you inject more play into your community or group?

2. Explore ways to play. Home school educator, Paula Russell, who incorporated a lot of play into her teaching, says, "Leave room for silliness and outrageous ideas and suggestions. Try improvisation, theater games, and physical activity to revitalize your brain."

Chapter 7

Seeding Intention

Do not worry if you have built your castles in the air.
They are where they should be.
Now put the foundations under them.
~ Henry David Thoreau, poet, author and naturalist

I ntention is a highly effective energy focuser. From heart-based intention fresh vision easily arises. From inspired vision ideas and
steps appear. From action manifestation is born. As Gabriele says,
"When you sit with focus and heart intention, a shockwave goes out on
the energetic level." Heart-centered intention is an energetic signal that
lays the foundation for manifestation.

The intention of my community is first and foremost the intention
to experience a greater realization of oneness at all levels. This intention is the force that directs us. I can almost hear the Disney tune, "It's
a Small World," as I write this. As corny as that may seem, I love Walt
Disney's intention to create the "happiest place on Earth." Perhaps the
call now is to intend something more expansive, like making Earth the
happiness planet in the galaxy. We're pretty far from that ideal; do you
think we can do it?

If we are to succeed, clear intention is necessary. Only then is the portal to conscious possibility wide open. Heart-centered intention helps make you aware of opportunities, processes and people that are in alignment with it. I believe intention lays down an energetic runway that helps you to more easily "land" your projects and plans.

Intention is an invitation for conscious unfolding to begin. As Chinese Humanistic Buddhist monk Master Hsing Yun says, "Intention is the core of all conscious life. Conscious intention colors and moves everything." As we connect to intention, we move community forward as an expression of our energy and the energy of those who join us in intentional play.

Seeding a collective field of energy

You may already be noticing that your dreams are not yours alone. We are connected to each other's dreams and intentions as never before — like a hive of bees doing a perfect dance of tuned-in creation. This connection helps us notice resources that aid in community building and group formation. It helps us come together to support each other in myriad practical and energetic ways.

Intention activates energy on both seen and unseen levels. Through intuitive awareness we are able to tap into "live" connections rather than getting misdirected by trying to plug into dead connections. For instance, when I was running my crowdfunding campaign I sent out an electronic press release about it. In my past, public relations had been a very successful career for me. Yet, I could tell immediately that there was zero energy attached to that press release; I had basically tried to plug in to a dead connection that was no longer live for me. What's live? The networks of people that I've nurtured for years through a newsletter and social media are live. My girlfriend networks are live. These networks are where my intentions connect much more easily, and where opportunities show up in the moment.

Live, heart-centered connections are how new community is being propelled worldwide by collective vision, inspiration, and especially through technology. People are tapping into the oneness field with more ease than our logical mental minds would allow in the past. When you align with another person the connection will be strong and you won't hesitate to reach out to them. In fact, you will feel happily compelled to contact them and create innovative dynamics. You will share knowledge and find new ways to support one another.

Our heart-centered connections are linking us in dynamic ways that aren't visible, too. We are energetically linking up. Many people around the planet are having the same impulses toward community creation that I am having. Likewise, there are people feeling heart urges in specific areas similar to yours. These seen and unseen energy connections will speed along and magnify outcomes, which then organically become outcomes for all.

Collective manifestation shift:
From limited to boundless

Since the day that my retreat center dream shifted to a vision of new community, I have come to realize that spiritually and energetically I AM the village. There is no separation between myself, my community partners, and what we create from heart-centered energy. This I AM automatically encompasses WE ARE. The same will be true for you as community co-creators. You inhabit and live the energy of what you create and what you engage with. It is an energetic projection of you.

In this way, creation is very personal. It is both play and responsibility. We cannot create and then pretend we are not the creation that has sprung from us (even though we might wish to). Outward reality not only reflects us, it is us. This desire for new community that is sprouting up around the globe is a reflection of our desire to come together in unity rather than divisiveness. Each group is an aspect of All That Is. The change seeds being sprinkled in the collective consciousness field are countless, and many will take root and bloom.

Perhaps that is why the idea of creating an entire village has felt like the most natural thing in the world. What has been even more surprising is that I immediately felt like it was more possible (easier even) to create a community than it would be to organize resources for a retreat center. This strong sense of ease feels like a signpost pointing to the truth that new community is greatly needed by the world. Rather than needing a retreat because we are burned out by busyness, distraction, and pointless work, community vision, participation and contribution affirms our ability to make a difference.

Collective Manifestation Blueprint Exercise: Intention Seeds

You might have lots of ideas about what to do with your precious life energy. The trick is discerning what wants to seed now! Intuition is a great discernment tool.

1. Think of each intention you have as a seed. Then take 15 minutes to journal about or intuitively answer the following questions. Trust the first answers that come to your mind:

   * What are the intention seeds I'm meant to plant now?

   * Which ideas are no longer relevant?

   * What intention seeds might I hold on to for later?

   * Have I connected heart energy to my dream?

   * Am I ready to focus on putting a foundation under my dream?

   * In what ways am I still allowing my ego mind to dictate my life plan?

2. If you are doing this as a group activity, complete the questions and then share the information.

3. From your answers do any simple steps come to mind? For instance, is there a step you can take to more fully connect heart energy to your intention?

4. Take at least one step to honor the intention planting you are meant to do.

—◦⊗◦—

7-Point I AM Heart Credo:

Collective manifestation is about creating as one dynamic force. Aim to be fully engaged and enthusiastic. Intend to experience beautiful flow even as you are processing and integrating personal life lessons at all times. Trust your ability to function effectively as an individual and as part of collective manifestation.

For instance, co-creators of New Village 22 align with the following heart-centered intentions to guide personal and group dynamics. Even living in different parts of the world, we are already the community we set out to establish. Intention is our magnetic time/space organizer. You may choose to integrate such heart-centered intentions for your own community or to define your own I AM/WE Are intentions.

1. **I AM/WE ARE receptive heart consciousness.** Consciousness facilitates wide-awake intent, true discernment, and clear choice-making. This is a commitment to tune into wisdom and love at all times for both personal growth and for the benefit of new community.

2. **I AM/WE ARE fertile heart space.** Expanded creativity requires opening one's heart space for fresh visions to seed themselves. Small blocks and big changes are beacons signaling areas for release and for growth. Open heart space is fertile ground for the entry of inspired ideas, the perfect companions, and remarkable connections to the world of energy flow. Allowing for expanded creativity requires a break from old mental attachments. (I even let go of my old friend ambition in order for a new vision to fill the empty space. It was a little like leaving my mental "field" fallow in order to enrich my heart field for new growth and fresh possibilities.) This

allowing for emptiness is part of developing trust in the inevitable cycle of evolution and dissolution.

3. **I AM/WE ARE surrendered heart.** Surrendering to not knowing all the answers is one of the most potently creative things we can do. Grace follows surrender, bringing about something wholly new, beyond social conditioning and habitual expectation. From surrender one may enter an open-ended system — an infinity system constantly generating and circulating remarkable variations of light, love and levity. When we release the need to predict how it all turns out, magic occurs.

4. **I AM/WE ARE multidimensional heart potential.** As multidimensional beings, we each have access to mental, emotional and spiritual states of being. Via a flexible perspective, emotional evolution, dream work, and spiritual focus we expand potential layer by layer. Such shifts reverberate throughout all levels of our being and through the life force of community. This willingness to play, this tuning in to various levels of awareness, gives birth to new co-creative brilliance.

5. **I AM/WE ARE a self-validating heart system.** I/we cannot fail, lose or be beaten. We win with each breath that holds the power of love, forgiveness and compassion. Such openness is not about not winning over another, or being in competition at all. As an open and self-validating heart system we choose to release social conditioning of comparison, constrictive life roles, and all fears of unworthiness. There is no fail, only progress. There is no loss, only learning. There is no beaten, only collaboration and co-creation.

6. **I AM/WE ARE one at heart with All That Is.** Our mission is to mirror in physical form the awakened unified field that we are. This is a field of expansive creative freedom, optimal energy flow, intrinsic meaning, easy connection, and nurtured spirit. We align to each

other and to All That Is with a bountiful heart committed to joy for all. Rather than controlling creation, we step into one flourishing heart. As above, so below; inner and outer walls dissolve. We are permeable beings giving and receiving at all times.

7. **I AM/WE ARE light and love.** As beings of light and love we are fluid possibility. With ego-mind no longer at the helm, a limitless future propels potent creation guided by soul design.

Collective Manifestation Blueprint Exercise: I AM/WE ARE intentions

1. Work with your group to outline intentions that align individual and group intention, while bringing focus to the purpose for creating community, and the effect you hope to have in the world.

Sample statements:

I am/we are love	I am/we are joy	I am/we are freedom
I am/we are justice	I am/we are change	I am/we are harmony
I am/we are caring service	I am/we are devotion	I am/we are grace under pressure
I am/we are strength	I am/we are fairness	I am/we are dynamic flow
I am/we are fertility	I am/we are gratitude	I am/we are harmony
I am/we are abundance	I am/we are opportunity	I am/we are brilliance
I am/we are innovation	I am/we are security	I am/we are bold voicing
I am/we are authenticity	I am/we are humor	I am/we are goodness
I am/we are wise energy	I am/we are synchronicity	I am/we are activism

I am/we are contribution

I am/we are science

I am/we are learned

I am/we are oneness

I am/we are receptive

I am/we are music

I am/we are visionary

I am/we are imagination

I am/we are wellness

I am/we are analytical

I am/we are acceptance

I am/we are supporters

I am/we are effective action

I am/we are life celebration

I am/we are generosity of spirit

I am/we are unified purpose

I am/we are performance

I am/we are spirit in action

Your primary I AM/WE ARE intentions:

1.

2.

3.

4.

5.

6.

7.

2. Discuss the following with your group:

* What WE ARE statements resonate most?

*   How might these WE ARE intentions/beliefs boost collective manifestation?

*   How might self-identifying I AM statements diversify what you can accomplish as a group?

*   Do your WE ARE statements center around a specific theme like heart, innovation, healing, physical experience, or service?

*   How might WE ARE statements empower your community's presence and communications to the outer community?

*   Will clarity around these intentions affect how your group proceeds? If "Yes," how?

Chapter 8

Nurturing Shared Success

It's not your differences that make you special...
What makes you special is that you are each Love Incarnate.
This connects you all, binds you all together.
~ Nora Herold, channel and healer

Y ou are each vehicles of light. You are each are here to channel wisdom, knowing, creativity and love in your own way. Our
individual lives have conspired to bring us to this point in history, but not for some individual glory. Instead, we are here now for
some collective brilliance that could not come into being any other way.
From this point forward we will view success as a shared reality.

The old paradigm has shifted and the energy around old societal
structures continues to disband. Things are in flux. Possibilities have
not solidified and this is good news. Creating intentional community
helps to define and give form to the new emerging paradigm.

From fresh discernment you can make new choices in line with
your values, needs and intentions. If hanging onto the old way of doing
things is no longer a controlling factor, groups can enact from a playful
heart center in which imagining the impossible, risk-taking and doing
the unusual becomes highly magnetic.

Collective manifestation shift:
From ego ambition to heart aspiration

If you are reading this you are at the forefront of this movement. Communities that advance harmony, health and happiness through creative vision outside the status quo are vital to a thriving populace and planet. Whereas old ego-based ambition tended to create imbalance and to dispirit, new heart-based aspiration seeks balance and to uplift.

Heart aspiration allows us to share the open space we've created in our minds, hearts and lives with others who are also seeking to occupy an empowered reality. We become human bridges to new potential as we create opportunities for ourselves and others at the same time. This highly fluid energy-exchange dynamic might show up as the exchange of information, as the connection of people online who need to know about one another or as in-person support and alliances. As social media "connector "Suzette Sommer says, "You never could have had these conversations before. It's a way of seeing community in a whole different way. We each get to initiate and participate in the communities we need. We can pool resources and cross promote each other's causes."

In an ideal world, businesses are communities that inspire and nurture talent, too. Megan Gaiser was one of the first female CEOs in the gaming industry, and is now a co-creator of Contagious Creativity. What she found during her fifteen years in the industry was that as exciting as the technical innovations were, true creative potential was not being tapped. "Creativity and collaboration are now two of the most important skillsets in the 21st century, and yet, creative cultures, remain few and far between in corporate America." She believes this is why one of the most lucrative and influential industries is suffering from an inability to mature. "It's a lack of wisdom in leadership," she states.

According to Megan, traditional leadership and a competitive work environment of bullying, manipulation and defensive, closed-minded brain storming, requires that "we show up as our shallow self, versus our full self." That competitive environment is no longer sustainable and certainly will not move us forward in innovation that changes the world for the better. Gaiser, like many others is being called to operate in the world from consciousness, cooperation and collaboration. As she so beautifully puts it, "Gutsy, collective co-creation is the freedom to claim our true brilliance, power and visionary skills."

As an example of how co-creation and collaboration work best, Megan shares the story of how when she launched the first Nancy Drew game at Her Interactive, her entire team approached everything as a fun mystery to be solved, like the game they created. "Curiosity was ever present. We found clues and new evidence all the time. Interrogating suspects was a daily routine. I was constantly learning in the moment. We ignored the naysayers and took smart risks." She is bringing this playful approach to her latest endeavor to creating inspiring games and facilitating creative culture change within the gaming industry. Her goal is to welcome more diversity in leadership and participation from thought leaders across industries to "energize minds and delights hearts."

Shared success begins by waking up to the remarkable benefits of re-evaluating any business, societal, cultural or familial dysfunction that has been accepted as normal up until now. Shared success means discovering together how to break away from the status quo and how to be a cohesively inspired unit that produces creativity that borders on the miraculous.

In the most foundational terms, co-creativity and collaboration is about approaching all areas of one's life as a shared endeavor. As Megan affirms, "Co-creativity means starting to practice what it means to really be human."

Collective Manifestation shift:
From energy suck to energy exchange

The balanced exchange of energy in/energy out is important to collective manifestation. The nature around you and within your own body is based on such an exchange. Here are some tips for being more conscious of maintaining such a balance.

1. Be mindful of the energy you are working with and remember the gifts you bring into this lifetime and into your projects.

2. Accept and tap into the energy already present. Tap into that which you already are, and use it as "clay" for the project.

3. Tap into connections with people who are lit up by the idea of collaboration and creativity. They are most likely to return your enthusiasm with their own passion.

4. Feel the frequency that puts you into contact with Sacred Source. Notice synchronicities like meeting the right person at the right time.

5. Learn to *be* the flowing frequency that manifests reality. This means identify resistance and minimize it. When do you withhold your brilliance and when does it easily bloom?

6. Align with each member of your community through open communication.

7. Don't worry about how you will get to some end point. At the early stages of community development all is ground for possibility. Practice holding open space for the unimaginable.

8. Picture the energy exchange happening in your group (see exercise)

Collective Manifestation Blueprint Exercise:
Energy Flow and Community Spirit

1. Answer the following questions:

   * What are the gifts you bring into your community, group or collective project?

   * What energy is already present that you can tap into? Is there a path of least resistance?

   * What has occurred within your group dynamic that indicates you are aligned with the spirit of your community or the group you are creating?

   * If you were to picture the "spirit of your community," what would it look like? Compile words that capture its essence. Or try drawing, painting, collaging, or using various materials to build a representation of this spirit.

2. Once you complete this process, note what you intuited about your community spirit.

————

Collective Manifestation Blueprint Exercise:
Heart-Centered Progress Checkup

As with any process, it's important to periodically evaluate what has been accomplished. Keeping a record of your activities and what you learned from them is a great way to do this. We do this with our meditation process (see Appendix 2). We record our individual experiences and combine them, along with feedback, and the key points of learning.

This generates cohesiveness. Everyone understands where we are in our process and when the next step or activity will take place.

1. Check in with your group. Ask members:

    *   Do you understand our intentions, values and purpose?

    *   Is everyone clear about our pillars of focus?

    *   Is everyone getting the experience they had hoped for?

    *   Has each person expressed clearly how they would like to use their skills, talents or gifts?

    *   What is your perspective of group success?

    *   Are there other ideas/solutions to address issues?

    *   Are there any ideas-topics-areas of interest that might be explored?

    *   Is there additional feedback?

2. Based on this review, choose heart-centered next steps.

Chapter 9

Anchoring in Love Currency

Without heart in all its forms and guises, life becomes sterile and frozen. We are not part of the whole, we are the whole.
~ Sarah Varcas, intuitive astrologer

In the context of new intentional community, any discussion of currency or economic change begins with the realization that the personal energy we exchange is the most important factor in our sense of abundance and plenty.

If we have learned anything from these tumultuous times, it's that the energy of competition and greed is as unstable as a foundation of sand. On the other hand, the currency of love is an infinite resource that endures beyond circumstance and situation. It cannot be diminished or ravaged. The currency of love only grows more expansive the more it is unchained from the bonds of fear. When we align with the expansiveness of what can be created through vision, devotion, imagination and engagement, we are in alignment with love currency.

Unconditional love is the essence of All That Is. Unconditional love is pure potential, so why not use it as a currency of exchange? This currency of love values all contribution and acknowledges systems of plenty. In such a system of balanced exchange nothing is lost. We give as naturally as we receive. This is a new way to view income. For instance, in our meditations the currency we receive reveals itself as new levels of seeing, listening, sensing and understanding. In our day-to-day community work, what each individual brings as skill and participation is what we value as in-coming energy. In this way this income is what we start with rather than what is earned as an end result of process or productivity. This is the energy of plenty.

This idea is radically different from our current economic system that is based on the energy of scarcity and not "enough-ness." The outcome of this sense of lack is a surfeit of "stuff." This stuff gets created detached from need or integral value. This is a waste of energy that creates enormous material waste and weighs us down energetically by its useless presence. This is just one example of non-essential, non-beneficial production/activity.

Collective scarcity-thinking is generally expressed by fears and insecurities like:

✳ Do I have enough?

✳ Will there ever be enough for everyone?

✳ If I have more than enough does someone else have less?

✳ Am I good enough to earn more?

✳ How do I now when enough is enough?

✳ Do others think I'm good enough?

✳ How do I hang onto enough?

Love currency, on the other hand, is energy born of the intention not to let fear limit one's sense of worthiness. Love currency is faith that you are supported by the Universe, that you are connected to Source, that there is enough for everyone.

I've had many clients and friends tell me during challenging times that what they needed always showed up just when they really needed it. They didn't know how it was going to happen, but it did. This is an example of love currency that is already available to us. Through generosity and compassion we help each other to manifest well-being on the planet.

Collective Manifestation Blueprint Exercise:
Charging Your Love Currency

Through our open-hearts we have the power to manifest a new economic reality individually and collectively. Even before your community is created there are ways to practice increasing your love currency.

1. **Find your riches in relationships**. The more you tap into your relationship resources, your people income, the stronger your support network becomes. You'll meet the right people at the perfect time. Relationship riches make you more adaptable to changing circumstance and present you with more opportunities. You would not be attracted to community if you did not believe that people are a valuable currency.

2. **When you're feeling lack, extend support to others**. When you take the focus off your lack and put it on your infinite wealth - your ability to give - you step back into your love essence. This empowers any group effort to effect change and to find satisfaction in how one positive step sends many ripples of energy outward.

3. **Practice holding your true worth**. By setting the intention to appreciate your innate worth, to love yourself and others

unconditionally, you increase your ability to hold your value no matter whom you are dealing with. Feel your worth from the heart, not as a test of wills (i.e, "I'm better than you" thinking). You know when you've created a stable sense of self-worth when changing circumstances don't greatly alter how you feel about yourself. You're able to observe them with more neutrality.

4. **When you feel fear, try shifting to a feeling of love**. This could be love for your family, love of your good health, love of your inherent talents, love for your spouse, love of a pet or animal, love of laughing, love of a sunny day, love of the smell of jasmine, love of a good meal. Feelings of love enable you to be a pollinator of progress, which is really one of the core manifestations we seek, that feeling of contribution and of having a positive effect.

Megan Gaiser knows about shifting out of fear. When the economy took its latest dip, she recognized that she was not at her best and had lost the cohesive flow of the group energy she had fostered as a leader. "I started to learn how to fully apply myself to live in the moment, how to learn to renounce fear. I thought I 'd mastered that in the past, but there's nothing like a big, scary economy-tanking challenge to remind me I needed to learn more to keep creative flow at all times."

5. **Send love to nature**. This includes sending love to the Earth, to the sky, the wind, the sea, to flora and fauna. The more you do so, the more you feel your connection to abundance.

Each of these steps helps you to anchor love in your life, in your communities, and on this magnificent planet.

Collective manifestation shift:
From a calculating economy to a customizable economy

Local economies and people's relationship to money is changing. It's as if many people simultaneously woke up and realized that the money game they'd been playing was no fun anymore. So they've opted to play diverse, more interesting games around exchange.

Many questions are being posed such as: "Can a global economy exist without money?" and "How do we create new systems for getting our material needs met?" Various new economies seek to replace, augment, and serve as a transition out of the old money paradigm. This creative surge in currency alternatives is another area in which humans are proving to be very resourceful.

There are varying perspectives about the dynamic taking place. In a September 2010 McKinsley Quarterly article titled, "Creating Value in the Age of Distributed Capitalism," Shoshana Zuboff, former professor of business administration at Harvard, calls important shifts in economic paradigms "economic mutations." She writes, "The leading edge of consumption is now moving from products and services to tools and relationships enabled by interactive technologies." Such mutations come about when businesses or industries don't make products or services available that people want at a price they can afford. Mutations also come about because businesses intent on maintaining control of specific information or product segments fail to recognize that customers increasingly want access to customizable products and services that they can access directly. Technology, via the iPod, famously made music selections customizable and instantly available through digital downloads.

Technological accessibility is an economic game-changer. Increasingly, more people are finding interesting ways to get their material needs by connecting with others via the Internet. Collaborative-style economies are becoming more and more prevalent. Goods like cars, tools and toys can be borrowed. Services can be bartered. Couches and bedrooms are available for short-term and extended stays. Clothes consignment has gone digital. This new adaptable economy thrives on social gain rather than financial gain.

Raja Choudhury is a creative director of successful digital and social campaigns in New York, London and New Delhi. He points out, "There are many social and web-based trends such as bartering, virtual money, alternative business corporations, the great non-profit revolution, innovation hubs, and crowd sourcing that can help us in our quest to make economics more spiritual and open. I am optimistic that these emerging trends will slowly parallel and perhaps even replace current banking, equity investment and capital flow models."

Some individuals are opting to make significant breaks from traditional capitalism and to highlight the greater value of security one finds in community. Irish activist and writer Mark Boyle is known as the "moneyless man." Once a student of economics, he eloquently points to the societal problems that have ensued from money replacing community as our source of security. In 2007, he founded online The Freeconomy Community based on unconditional giving and a pay-it-forward philosophy. Rather than direct exchange or barter, participants give what they have to others in terms of skills, goods or space. Then the recipients likewise pay the favor forward by freely giving of their own talents, products and services. In his 2011 TEDx O'Porto speech, Boyle said that the prevailing economic system is destructive because it both encourages disconnection from nature and from what we consume, which has significant social and ecological repercussions.

Over its thirty year history, the spiritual eco-community of Damanhur in Italy has developed and refined its own economic system that combines free enterprise with communal sharing for its 600 members. As a post titled, "Social and Economic Model," on the *Damanhur Community Blog* explains, communal plenty is "expressed in houses and land, schools and services, art and gardens, forests and meeting spaces, health and wellness, as well as a sense of belonging and security, and attention for the individual, from an economic and human point of view."

Arthur Brock, co-founder of Emerging Leader Labs (ELL), and New Currency Frontiers, believes that reevaluating what we accept as currency is essential to the development of new community. As he states, "Learning the power of currencies enables us to re-encode social DNA, rewire social nervous systems, enhance the perceptual systems and upgrade the collective intelligence of our social organisms."

In the development of his community-based incubator project in New York State, Brock reports that the ELL community has operated almost solely on a gift economy. "There has been negligible financial contribution because we've never asked anyone to contribute financially. We receive value in food, shelter, social strength and community without money changing hands. And we've spent some of our own money on things (supplies, materials, and foodstuffs that could not be supplied by local farmers) to fill in some of the gaps in community support." Brock and his partner Eric Harris-Braun are committed to providing a model for world-change projects that does not involve significant financial capital. As he stated, "We think it's important that we walk our talk to be sure it can be done that way."

Futurist and global-society visionary Jacque Fresco is the creator of an extraordinary social proposal called The Venus Project. On his website, www.thevenusproject.com, he states the following about the possibility of building a resource economy:

> To better understand the meaning of a resource-based economy consider this: if all the money in the world were destroyed, as long as topsoil, factories, and other resources were left intact, we could build anything we choose to build and fulfill any human need. It is not money that people need; rather, it is free access to the necessities of life. In a resource-based economy, money would be irrelevant. All that would be required are the resources and the manufacturing and distribution of the products.

These community activists and designers address the intrinsic need and desire for economic innovation. This is a trend toward depending on each other rather than depending on how much money we can manage to make, or how much someone is willing to pay us or loan us. It gives us back our power, and reasserts the power of relationship, which is based on our heart connections to others and to the generous living world around us.

Valuing heart-centered contribution

Wouldn't you love live in a world in which people are doing what makes their heart sing and contributing to community in meaningful ways that elevate esthetics, cultural richness, societal interaction, and community spirit?

When we enjoy the freedom of contributing our gifts in the most inspired and useful form possible, then our societies will reflect values of connection and commitment to creation over consumption. Contribution to society should be expansive, inclusive. We self-limit by allowing corporations, marketers and advertisers to determine what we consider valuable. Intentional community can address this issue by coming up with new ways to validate a wide range of human endeavors. We can shift out of buying habits into economic support for all the activities we value. Each community can create a new economic recipe for how they innovatively do that.

A May 2013 research paper, published through The Brookings Institution, titled "How Millennials Could Upend Wall Street and Corporate America," contends that the values of Millennials is likely to significantly impact the current economic structure. The authors, Dr. Morley Winograd and Michael Hais, point to Millennials' desire to advance the good of the group more than they care about fixating on individual success. The paper reports that Millennials value experiences over acquiring material goods, and they value the "ability to build communities around shared interests rather than geographical proximity, bridging otherwise disparate groups." Such findings affirm the societal shift that is apparent to diverse community-minded people of all ages and interests, who are already working toward significant economic changes for the good of all.

Women in Innovation, founded by leadership coach and innovator Kristiina Hiukka in 2011, is an online and live-event community that addresses the cultural "blind spot" of women not being seen as innovators in economy and technology. Kristiina says, "When women are not participating in the innovation economy we miss an opportunity to embrace and engage all human potential in solving global challenges." The Women in Innovation global community facilitates success for women with big ideas, and aims to bring about economic change in the world. Action to forward a more just and balanced economy is the best kind of heart currency.

What about the current economy seems unbalanced to you? How might this be addressed by your community? Currency systems don't need to be all one thing. In fact, it seems likely that there will be a layering of various exchange systems as we continue to transition into a more heart-centered mindset about economics and exchange currencies. Just as products and services are more customizable these days, intentional collective manifestation empowers us to create the customized systems that address economic limits and issues. Through the power of collective focus your group or community can create a more balanced exchange system that aims to generate what is most needed for individuals and for the group.

Fortunately, we live at a time when relatively new technology and economic models empower people to get their funding needs met in creative ways. Crowfunding was a featured player in our economic model to get this book out into the world. By going directly to a wide range of people interested in supporting various projects, I believe we'll see much more diversity in the innovations and projects people produce. Losing the hierarchy intrinsic to the current economic system is a good thing.

Marianne Williamson, who used crowdfunding to support her political campaign, stated in social media, "Some people believe it's naïve to think we can make love our new bottom line. What I believe is naïve is thinking human civilization as we know it will survive another 200 years if we do not." What this so beautifully points out is that love is the core of sustainable collective manifestation.

New Village 22 Blueprint Exercise: Community Currency

1. Outline your community's ideas and feelings related to economy. Some questions to get you started:

    *   What community values will lead your intentions around economy creation?

    *   What currencies will you exchange?

    *   What will be the basis of your economy?

    *   Will you seek community sponsorships?

    *   Is your group interested in creating a moneyless economy?

    *   Are you interested in crowdfunding as a revenue generator?

    *   Do you wish to create a community that is off the grid?

    *   How might a "blended" economic system work?

    *   Will individual members be responsible for bringing income into the community?

    *   How will shared economic responsibilities be handled?

Chapter 10

New Earth Incubation

God's love is manifest in the landscape as in a face.
~ John Muir, naturalist

A n evolved and living relationship to Earth and all beings is fundamental to human progress. It's vital to realize that we are in an incubation period in which we have an opportunity to newly define our connection to the natural world. Through the recognition that everything holds spirit, you have a chance to experience an authentic relationship with the world around you.

Celebrating nature is but one of the shifts that are necessary for healing our relationship to ourselves and this precious planet. Activism on behalf of nature aims to shift us from the brink of destroying that which nurtures and supports human life, to a new respectful relationship. Such shifts help to bring us into a daily experience of our oneness with all. This is the very energetic foundation of the establishment of intentional community.

Heart-centered intentional community is about embodying new waves of energy to heal the emotional separation and the mental compartmentalizing that makes it easy to rationalize and justify any endeavor that means more convenience, comfort, and financial success.

The intent of New Village 22 group, and perhaps yours, is to co-create from the viewpoint that humans are not the only beings of importance. As humans we benefit exponentially by seeing ourselves as part of a whole and living world — a world that itself has a living relationship to other beings and planets in the universe.

Collective Manifestation shift:
From existing on the Earth to being One with Earth

As you begin your community or join a community project, make the simple yet powerful intention to harmonize your heart energy with the heart energy of Earth and all beings, to step into greater potential than ever before. By valuing the input and permission of all beings, believe that you will arrive at different, more fascinating junctures. Trust that you will naturally come to innovative, multidimensional community solutions that address how to responsibly and happily co-exist with Earth in its context as one planet in the cosmos.

Heart-centered intentional groups anchor in this love energy in myriad ways and forms. New Village 22 recognizes that Earth is alive with its own magnificent inner nature, and miraculous eco-systems that can thrive in cooperation with us. With energy being one of our pillars of focus, we are committed to actively interacting energetically with the spirit of land, property and all things built upon Earth. We acknowledge that the relationship we have to Earth is central to sustainability and responsible energy use.

Already groups and communities are co-creating their own Earth and nature-related niches. Some are animal and agricultural based, some are about saving the rain forest. Others are focused entirely on renewable energy sources. Each is vital to the reclamation of our true relationship potential with Earth and all its beings.

What do you intend in regard to your relationship to nature? How can you co-create with nature as an active participant? What is the least you could do to express higher potential? What is the most you desire to do?

Author David Christopher recommends in his book *The Holy Universe*, "Find a place on Earth, even a small one, that is in need of care. Take care of it. Learn what you can from it." There are many ways to learn from Earth, but as with any relationship, we first have to ask what is needed and observe or sense how Earth replies.

Land and property dynamics

What my own community group is envisioning and manifesting is the antithesis to the heartless development I grew up with in Southern California during the sixties and seventies. I vividly recall the bulldozing and cutting into the land without regard for the Earth as a living being. Track by track, the natural landscape was covered by houses. I felt both extremely lucky to grow up in Southern California and a deep sadness each time I saw the bulldozers begin their destruction. I recall thinking that it was like Mother Earth was getting another mastectomy. How many could she bear?

This imbalance of man versus Earth continues. You see it all around you. It is time to create a new sense of true home in which all beings are valued as sacred. Co-create from a heart-based vision of your village home. Tap into the impulse to belong, to give and receive in new relationship to others and the world you inhabit. Such a focus facilitates bringing respect and reverence to communal interaction and co-creation.

If you are reading this book, you may be eager to take part in the righting of the imbalances in the world's ecosystems and social systems. You are ready to rebirth yourself as a caring creator that collaborates.

In honor of a more conscious relationship with Earth, you can choose new ways of interacting with the energies of land and property.

For those of you interested in creating a community with a physical location, you can even approach construction in a manner that recognizes the land as a conscious, energy-exchanging being. Being in relationship with Earth means recognizing and acknowledging that there exists the energy dynamics inherent in any healthy relationship. These dynamics include:

* Appreciating one's connection to Earth as to another living entity, and being in gratitude for how the relationship adds to the quality of living each day.

* Respectful and permission-based interaction (one of New Village 22's core values). This acknowledges that rather than imprinting all our desires upon Earth, we understand that the Earth itself, that the spirit of place, may inform decisions and choices.

* Heart inquiry. Sincerely asking questions like: "What does Earth want?" or "What does this property need?"

* Listening and being a caring witness to the needs of Earth (as a life partner), and being in recognition of what helps it to flourish.

* Observing unhealthy relationship patterns and helping to heal energetic blocks when possible.

* Celebrating the sacred nature of the relationship.

As we are witnessing, Earth is neither an endless resource, nor a bottomless dumping ground. If we are to live in harmony within our communities, we must begin by establishing a loving relationship with earth. In co-creative cooperation, it's critical to aim to give as we receive at every step of the process. We can send heart energy to Earth in meditation; we can be good stewards of the land we call home; we can be more like naturalist John Muir, loving and enjoying the miracle of the natural world as it heals us.

Connecting to nature can be a simple daily practice. Among her many talents (cultural anthropologist, public health expert, student of Chinese healing arts) Karen Joy Fletcher is a Qigong teacher, and daily practice enthusiast. She is one with her environment wherever she is, whether it's in a remote area of China (where she becomes part of a healing community) or by a lake in urban Seattle. Recently she told this story about a beautiful and unexpected group Qigong session. "While walking around the lake I stopped by a secluded point of land that jets out into the water with some beautiful trees hanging over the water's edge. I started doing a self-healing qigong practice. I closed my eyes and followed my body's movements. After a few minutes I opened my eyes to make sure I wasn't going to step or fall into the lake as I was moving around. To my surprise there were eight Canadian geese all spread out in front of me in the shallow water. Each was cleaning themselves, their beaks buried under a wing, or stretching down to scratch their chest feathers, or turned with their beaks rustling some back feathers — all busily doing their own version of self-care or what looked like a Canadian Goose-style of self-healing Qigong! And then as I finished, they did, too, and slowly swam away as a group!" This is a wonderful example of how embodying your own joy and passion easily aligns you with other inhabitants of the natural world, and allows the magic of life to show up.

At any point you can live your Earth-related values. You can use the practical blueprints and intuitive tools in this book to be in conscious relationship with land and property — whether it's in relation to an apartment building or a single-family home. You can engage in energy clearing of property, interior beautification, and gardening. You may use your talents and gifts to facilitate *living* relationships with land, gardens, and structures. It's all about anchoring more love into Earth in any way you choose and enjoy.

Collective manifestation shift:
From isolation to belonging

People who own and co-own land and buildings can choose to be evolved co-creators contributing to a revitalized heart-connected society. For instance, this could be changing the typical landlord-renter relationship to one of shared community. Rather than looking for tenants to occupy residential units, people might be invited to belong to authentic community (much as the co-housing communities set out to do).

New community is not about coming home and shutting our doors against the rest of the world. I've seen plenty of so-called luxury apartments and condos in which the workout rooms and common areas sit empty and lifeless — the smoke and mirrors of a "high quality" life. Without heart-centered connection even the supposedly best space remains energetically empty and dead.

Midlife for so many Baby Boomers has the potential to profoundly influence this aspect of property ownership. For instance, I spoke with a woman who was recently widowed. The question that she is trying to live into is: "What new form will a sense of belonging take?" She has friends who own an apartment building and there have been conversations about creating connected community using this residential form. It provides the privacy individuals desire, and with social restructuring, could provide opportunities for a shared life experience that makes use of the participants' knowledge, wisdom, skills and desire to make an impact.

The reasons people find themselves without community connections are varied. As social-media activist Suzette Sommer observes, "People today find themselves lacking community for many reasons: the fact that half of our adult population is single at any given time; the fact that Americans typically move every few years, disrupting everyday ties; our economic downturns frequently force job changes and relocations, and even aging is a factor, as retirement from a career often brings with it the loss of routine and community within a company or industry. All of these situations and more leave many people longing for more stable relationships, more connections and more meaningful interactions day-to-day."

Perhaps just a slight shift in perspective is all that is needed to address these disconnects. Apartments for students can be expanded into centers for innovation and dynamic community involvement. Perhaps a new viewpoint is all that is needed to shift retirement facilities into mentoring centers that take advantage of all the accumulated knowledge, experience and wisdom seniors can share. We have existing structures that can be used differently — by asking people how they want to connect, live and engage within these structures. We all need a place to live, why not make that part of the solution we seek to see in the world?

Collective Manifestation Blueprint Exercise: Land Ho!

1. Here are some questions for your group to consider in regard to transforming what already exists in terms of land and property into communities of sacred exchange and celebration.

    *   How-can an existing property (home, apartment, condo complex, multi-acre property, etc.) be transformed or further co-created to be more inclusive?

    *   Does the idea of finding and reinventing a "ghost town" appeal to you?

    *   How could property holdings become cooperative and heart-based?

    *   What would be necessary to reorganize outdated property-ownership models to reflect intention toward co-creation, beauty, giving place meaning, and inspiring a greater sense of belonging and joy?

* How do you hold space for what wants to unfold, while sharing what you "own" so that it too becomes representative of the global heart you are birthing?

* How can property owners reorganize their thinking and property management to reflect co-creation — every occupant feeling a part of creating something bigger than their own personal space needs?

* How could you energize or beautify current property you lease or rent? What would need to happen? Plant gardens or choose colors for painting interiors? Would you need to meet with owners to discuss this? What is your contribution — what is their contribution? Why would they be inspired to engage at a higher level than is normal?

* If an apartment building or condo complex becomes representative of a new model of what community can be, what energy work would you (or your group) be willing to do to pave the way for that?

* How could purchasing and developing tracks of land be part of the new Earth paradigm that benefits all?

* How could your community interact and engage with other communities?

* What is your idea or vision of living in harmony with the land?

* Is living off-grid appealing?

* What land or property related opportunities are you becoming aware of?

The clearer you are on these questions, the easier it will be to attract members to your new community group who aspire to facilitate changes that engender a more conscious relationship to land-property-housing and living structures.

New Village 22 community member Gabriele has wrestled with issues of property ownership and investment, and the complexities of sharing living space. For instance, she and her husband own an apartment complex that was easily attained, but then just sat with no energy seeming to be directed toward it. People moved out. Completing repairs proved difficult. As a result, they felt little enthusiasm for developing and improving the property. Yet, realizing that we are in a time of active participation with Earth, land, and property, Gabriele got clarity on questions such as those listed above, and found ways to either effectively inject energy in the property projects or consciously disconnect her energy. She states, "It feels right to live, love and work as if a conscious world community is already in place. We live as if it has all happened already by integrating all that we know into the shift that is on our doorstep right now. We are not separate; we can start to live the dream!"

Collective Manifestation Blueprint Exercise:
Location, Location, Location!

How a community's location facilitates group development is a world unto itself. Naturally, a group that stakes out its territory in a social-media environment is going to development differently than a group in which members interact face-to-face. It's a fascinating area for exploration.

For example, by beginning as a group that meets remotely and doesn't have a physical location, we are learning how to effectively connect our individual energies in a non-physical way. Also, we can leisurely play with what we can learn about advantageous land features and various geographic considerations that might impact an eventual physical community. When estuaries came up as a theme in our intuitive processes, Gabriele asked her guides: "What is important about an estuary?" The answer was that salinity is about crystals – which facilitate an optimized flow of information. "The water carries the vibes and the Earth hears it!" she explained. Such knowledge might facilitate specific activities and interaction with nature at such a location.

Grounding intention in Earth

Grounding intention through action is a key to nourishing community development and collective manifestation. I watched a video titled, *"Medieval Spanish ghost town becomes self-sufficient,"* about a community in Spain that started from a deserted medieval town. The co-creators approached the intense work of creating new community from ruins as an adventure. The freedom they had to build the community they wanted, unimpeded by modern "civilization," was their energetic well. This resulted in the acquisition of remarkable skills in everything from building construction to engineering a wind turbine. There were enough people, who adapted well to the intense hands-on community building, to keep the work progressing for decades.

Starting fresh, outside established societal structures, offers an open path to fulfilling one's vision for community. It is a chance to be experimental in an exciting way that thrives on flexibility and process, rather than figuring out how to fix or go around dysfunctional and static societal systems that are already in place. Our community has received information related to this through Gabriele's intuitive process, which enables her to communicate with the energy or "the spirit" of land, buildings and structures. She has received insights that a populace can be unconsciously suppressed by societal programming that gets encoded into the very buildings of cities. "What I clearly sensed was the suppressed, low consciousness in London — the enslavement of the buildings that have a 'keep our heads down or off with their heads' attitude — and the money-making machinery behind the whole property market in London, and how this keeps all consciousness under a dome of arrogance and greed."

Collective Manifestation Blueprint Exercise:
Where would you like your community to "live?"

1. As a leader of new community, that might have a physical location, consider the following questions:

   * What are your initial inclinations related to the location of your community?

   * What would be the advantages, if any, of having a physical location in light of your goals for the community?

   * What geographical features might be important to the successful realization of your new community?

   * What intuitive insights or clues are you receiving about location?

   * Are you planning on working within an established community? If yes, how does this align with your vision, values and goals?

   * How might you integrate your community structure/values with a larger community for the benefit of all?

Occupancy exchanges

Earthly property rebalancing also occurs through "occupancy exchanges." These exchanges of place and daily life reality are increasingly making residential habitation flexible and fluid. For instance,

Gabriele needed a vacation, and her sister-in-law had an apartment in Spain. Holding the intention for an occupancy exchange, Gabriele was quickly able to rent her flat in London to a couple who needed multiple rooms for themselves and their relatives for the same time period. Thus, everyone got the location they desired.

Even in the writing of this book, I easily connected with someone who wanted to make their home available, while they were on vacation in Mexico. I got a quiet place to write, they got a house/dog sitter. In such occupancy exchanges, everyone gets to experience a new environment, or a simple way to step out of one's comfort zone into something new.

This dynamic is being played out around the globe. People are exchanging and sharing their homes, their comfort zones, even their couches, with others who want to explore and experience life opportunities from a different location for a week, a month, or even for a year or more.

In addition, there is a trend of people leaving the security of home or a home base in exchange for a life of adventure and a chance to experience the greater world. People are giving up stationary properties for mobile ones — trailers and RVs, backpacks and open-ended itineraries. This seems to reflect a heart-based inclination and longing to get back into nature, to experience the world's wonders, to feel more alive, and to connect to new people. All of these scenarios enable people to more fully occupy and engage their lives in interesting and fluid ways.

The old paradigm of purchasing property merely to own and control more "earthly assets" is shifting to heart co-creation and respectful care and cooperation with the land.

Increasingly, as we collectively shift into heart guidance, I believe you'll see groups of people purchasing property in order to expand and share their passions and interests. Whether these life-enhancing pursuits result in creativity centers, alternative healing communities, teen hubs or more agricultural co-ops, they will organically make life better for everyone.

Such balanced interaction with the essence of place and space reflects our changing interaction with the world. Asking and understanding what is energetically "best" for the spirit of place facilitates the ease of creation and moves us humans into new realms of possibility. The land, the earth, the plants, can tell us what is best. A friend recently had a dream in which a field of wheat was interspersed with wild flowers, so that the wheat would not get bored. There's a magical logic to that!

This relating-to-the-environment dynamic has the power to form new societal pathways. Then it becomes easier and more "normal" for people to explore what it means to occupy, to share, to exchange, and to make room for others in a more vital and connected life experience. Perhaps as more people come to feel that their true safety comes from within, there's less need for comfort zones expressed by exterior square-footage.

As with all things, there is a polar opposite movement to get away from it all that has more to do with dis-connection, to closing down the heart rather than opening it up. I recently read a newspaper article about a 60-something man who was quietly buying up property in North Dakota in order to create a community where the old paradigm could be preserved (aka old white men in charge).

We're at a point in which releasing the traditional for expanded possibility is a key attraction to change. Likewise, I know several women around the age of 60 who are envisioning a time in the very near future in which it makes more sense to live with others than to live alone in a single family dwelling. This is not only a cost consideration. It's a question of community — of having privacy but not isolation, of sharing meals rather than losing connections, and of encouraging the ongoing creative development of all. It's an inclination toward support rather than separation from others. It's recognition that we all have more than enough to share. This is an energetic and active, heart-based vision in which everyone has a better shot at exploring and expressing their creative and spiritual potential, no matter their age.

What we know is that stuff doesn't buy security. On the other hand, sharing of oneself and exchanging of one's material goodness, does create a bridge into one's unlimited heart.

The power of ritual

Rituals are a natural way to interact with the land as a conscious being. Rituals are a way to experience more shared daily meaning. Ancient rituals were often tied to the seasons and fertility, and to divinity, and the stars. Rituals gave us a way to be connected to these systems. We can newly honor and integrate meaningful rituals into collective manifestation to affirm our connection to nature and how nature is a mirror for our own bodily systems. There are energetic alignments that organically spring from sharing sacred practices.

In the meditative visioning practice, we are using to establish an energetic foundation for our New Village 22 community, rituals like dances, songs, hand movements, and prayers have played a role in our development. These rituals often show up as an expression of joy, and as a way to move and direct energy with clear intention.

Additionally, ritual can be used to heal group conflicts, to honor group members, and to generate a greater sense of gratitude in what we have to celebrate. Ritual can transform mental intention into a sacred activity. Ritual, at its best, embodies heart inspiration and devotion.

Collective Manifestation Blueprint Exercise:
Establishing Rituals of Blessing and Celebration!

1. If you have not yet started your community, decide if you would like to incorporate a blessing or celebration into its kickoff.

2. Select a blessing you would like to use to open your community, or use the one below.

3. If your community is already established, discuss the power of rituals with your members and decide if you would like to create different blessings or celebrations for the various stages of your process.

4. You might use blessings or another ritual at the beginning of key junctures and then celebrate progress and accomplishment at the conclusion of phases. This will help to keep the bright spirit of your community alive.

Community Blessing

Alleluia, alleluia, alleluia.
From the grace of Source all goodness flows abundantly.
From the fertile soils of an open heart community rises.
From seeds of intention, community germinates new possibility.
From a willingness to engage, community grows strong.
From rich connections to all beings, community sends out new waves
of hope and love, gratitude and delight.

Blessed are the many hearts that are the force of change.
May we shine as a source of inspiration and plenty for all.

Blessed are the daring hearts that are the force of change.
May each community illuminate a new worldview of what is
possible to create, share and experience.

May all radiant communities give form to sacred brilliance.
In our oneness, we allow love to live us in peace, wellness and joy.
And so it is.

Chapter 11

Germination and Transformation

When we wonder, we manifest.
~ Joyce Anderson, author and parenting advocate

G ermination is the phase of community building that requires the most patience. It's easy to get mentally impatient and frustrated, and to lose focus. Yet, when you tune into the heart, you will find greater enjoyment in the journey. You will be mesmerized by what is unfolding both subtly and unmistakably.

Thus far, this book has discussed the practical and organizational aspects of collective manifestation that create an energetic foundation for community. These aspects have included:

* Identifying core values and member needs.

* Deciding on pillars of focus.

* Planting energetic seeds of intention.

*   Releasing ego-mind directives (limits) and opening to heart-mind brilliance.

*   Healing personal energy fields so that collective consciousness expands.

*   Grounding I AM/WE ARE essential aspects.

*   Appreciating what each community member brings to the manifestation process.

*   Connecting your heart energy to Earth heart.

*   Incubating a new permission-based relationship to Earth-land-property.

Germination is a multi-layered process. It is the time to nurture the sprouted intentions you set forth for yourself and your community. At germination energy can coalesce with nurturing or energy can become weakened from lack of care and heart attention. You should sense that energy has been activated and continues to gain momentum. Keep taking steps that reinforce your conscious vision.

This period also presents the opportunity to evolve specific areas that hold additional growth potential for all. These are areas that may not yet be obvious as they still need nurturing in order to breakthrough to the seen in order to more powerfully uplift the whole of humankind.

Areas for germination

I intuit that the following areas are still being germinated by community and by humanity in order for collective consciousness to advance further. The three key areas are:

1. **Sensing energy** — This is the seed of intuiting what exists beyond surface appearances and beyond surface interaction with the intent

to "read" the energy aligned with everything. For instance, you can sense the high or low health frequency of food and then from this discernment make wise choices based on the energy one perceives as being helpful or not. Sensing into the energy of various choices you can discern the path of least resistance. By learning to discern the sacred energy exchange you are always engaged with, you can better learn to unfold what you intend to manifest. You can engage life more fully and wisely. Training in discernment is the key to this sensing wisdom.

2. **The present mind** — This is the seed of living in the now moment. A simple approach to germination is to take a child-like attitude, and by engaging activities such as meditation as simple play. As the wise Joyce Anderson phrased it, "You can only play in the present." Germination occurs by directing one's thoughts with optimism, embracing a sense of wonder and exploration, and keeping open to new ideas and insights. The present mind is about movement and free-flowing imaginative brilliance. The present mind is tuned to sacred simplicity. By taking away what is mentally extraneous (like distractions), you experience manifestation unfolding as perfect flow. Rather than staying stuck in old patterns of thinking, and being attached to what we think life should look like, the present mind is available to perceive new paths and present possibilities.

3. **Self-love** — This is the seed of ease and grace, self-care and compassion, empathy and acceptance. It is perhaps the most difficult seed to germinate, yet the most essential to thriving heart-based communities. Self-love is acceptance of yourself as perfect in the now moment; it is recognition of your sacred and noble relationship to All That Is. Self-love requires letting go of narrow societal definitions of worth and aligning with your higher self that knows your true capabilities and life mission. Germinating the seed of self-love requires holding your heart open even when the mental mind resists. It requires holding steady the frequency of love no matter

the situation. We may mentally appreciate the truth that we are all equally valuable. Yet, until this truth drops into each of our hearts, it is lip service.

Collective Manifestation Blueprint Exercise:
What Needs To Be Germinated Guided Meditation

1. Gather your community group together for a live meditation. Alternately you can arrange a remote meditation that allows each person to individually meditate from their location at a pre-determined time, in order to energetically link.

2. Someone will need to read the meditation for the live group meditations. For remote meditations the meditation below can be pre-recorded or it may be read through and the process recalled during meditation.

3. If you are doing this meditation live, form a circle. Sit comfortably with your feet flat on the ground. Begin the meditation by taking a couple of relaxing breaths. Close your eyes. Feel into the presence of abundant heart space within your circle.

Guided meditation

Sense or imagine your group sitting in a circle facing each other. Begin to see the formation of light-bridges that connect your hearts to each other. Take a minute to really sense that your heart light is ignited; is flowing with easy joy.

Then notice that the circle begins to slowly turn clockwise. It is as if you are grounded, and yet seated on an invisible platform that is able to rotate. You understand that what needs to be germinated for your group is opening to you as you turn. It's like unlocking a vault. After three turns you accept that you have access to the wisdom of the earth. When the circle stops turning, you each imagine getting up to explore the "field" about you.

Your pace of exploration is your own — do this as quickly or as patiently as you desire, knowing that all is working in perfect timing. Explore until you sense that you need to uncover a particular seed for germination. Dig this seed out of the earth and bring it back to the group.

You are all again seated in your circle and you listen as each person explains what needs to be germinated for your community, showing you the seed they have uncovered. You may clearly hear them speaking or merely sense that they are offering their germination insights — which you will know about soon enough. After each person speaks they put their seed for germination in the center of the circle.

Then it's your turn to speak. You hear yourself very clearly talking about the seed you brought back. You might describe what this seed looks like and what the seed is called. You may describe its qualities. You explain why this particular seed is needed as you move forward with your community creation. When you are finished, place your seed in the center with the others.

Once again the circle turns, this time counter-clockwise. You see the seeds begin to sprout and to be reabsorbed by the earth's warm fertile soil. When each seed is replanted you give thanks for the perfection of this growth cycle. You join in a group blessing for these germination efforts on behalf of Earth and all humans.

When you are ready, open your eyes and make notes about what you learned during this process, and then share your experience with the other members of your group.

Collective manifestation shift:
From disconnected energy to activated potential

This initial phase of community creation is based on the acceptance that what is "behind the seen" is just as important as the seen. It's the understanding that to create heaven on Earth it's vital to consciously connect to the energy that becomes manifested reality. The phrase "as above so below" reminds us of the wholeness and innate energetic balance of everything.

The germination phase of intentional community building is the time to practice nurturing your mental intentions with heart energy. When you do this, you activate your potential and you germinate love, discovery, inventiveness, beauty, imagination, acceptance, adaptability, and compassion as part of your group development. Part Two of this book provides processes that enable you to be more aware of the energy that you both radiate and are aligned with. You begin to familiarize yourself with the manifesting energy you've already generated. You practice aligning internal energy with externally actions that boost individual and collective growth potential. You hold heart space for spontaneous manifestation.

Community development is ideally suited to developing both the practical and mystical qualities of manifestation. While you make yourself aware of what is being developed to address various community issues in the greater world and what can be done better, you can experiment with how to newly manifest better solutions. As you observe what is happening with education, home design, urban planning, sustainability, agriculture, alternative health, with bringing creativity and the arts to people of all ages, you learn to appreciate and expand your own remarkable capabilities that positively affect and contribute to a domino effect for good in the world.

Living a connected life is about paying attention to your dreams and to the dynamics being played out in your home and within your extended family. You will inevitably notice how what happens at the individual level is always being mirrored in collective consciousness.

In this way, you are constantly getting a preview of what is coming into manifested reality. That's why it is important to acquire the intuitive tools that allow you to be aware of the divine energies flowing through you — that can easily direct, support and guide your discovery and creation process.

This can feel both exciting and scary, as it is new territory for many to trust one's intuition fully. Getting used to opening up to the unknown teaches you how to balance excitement with being a little scared — how to allow these feelings to co-exist. Then as you continue to connect to possibility through your heart, as you invite alignment to your higher self, the fear dissipates.

Germinating the new you

Experiencing your true heart-centered self requires relinquishing mental control. This may require an inner agreement to trade control for spontaneity and inspiration. It usually requires the conscious release of old programming around what constitutes fulfillment, and ingrained ideas about what roles are innately most purposeful and important. It takes honesty with one's self about how you choose to stay stuck in habits of mind or action and how you may be attracted to self-sabotage.

If you are reading this, then perhaps you can accept that you chose this path of new community creation and new promise. You are indeed ready to detach from old programming. Yes, it may be tempting to run back to old comfort zones many times over. Yet, each time you do you will increasingly be confronted with the dead-end energy that occupies these old comfort zones. So each day, moment-to-moment, try again and again to live anew, to nurture the opportunities that are ready to emerge through your brilliance.

Seven signs that a new you is emerging

1. **Your focus has shifted from distraction to devotion.** You aren't as focused on the empty distraction that used to grab your at-

tention, like celebrity gossip, fashion fads, stock reports, and over-dramatized news reports. Instead you're directing your attention to innovations, inventions, creativity, nature, environmental projects, global health, human kindness heroes, sustainable home design, the aligning of science and spirit, and all manners of life richness.

2. **Your anti-consumer consciousness is strengthening.** You realize what a trap being a "good" consumer is. You are increasingly attracted and lit up by the idea of being a creator — by the activity of creating.

3. **You are an advocate for change.** You are ready to move way beyond-beyond the status quo! You're picking up on change ideas that can improve your life and empower the lives of others.

4. **Your heart is wide open.** You are experiencing waves of emotion. Sometimes you can explain these intense feelings, sometimes you're not sure where they are coming from. At times it feels like clearing, like a big release. Often emotions rise from a sense of gratitude you have generated. Your emotions are a channel for free-flowing heart energy.

5. **You hold high frequency.** This is important for self, for all beings, and for the planet. High frequency activities include: meditation and prayer, and playing in the unseen realms of energy, intention, vision and imagination. You align to the frequency of uplifting service, healing, creativity, and fresh life experience. As you master your own energy, you understand that your precious energy is yours to play with and direct — rather than letting it be hijacked or siphoned away by others.

6. **You balance reception and transmittal (or exertion).** This may include receiving great ideas and meeting with other

heart-aligned people to build on those ideas in the creation of fascinating projects and programs. This reception/transmittal balance naturally develops the "new" you that allows heart-spirit to lead or drive vision, and mind-body to embody and realize vision. This balance aligns to the belief that we are not here to change other people; we are only here to heal ourselves and shift others into a higher frequency. As Gabriele says, "I offer myself as a tuning fork for what wants to be seen in the light." Being authentically present to each other (and indeed to all beings) is the gift you give and receive with more and more grace.

7. **You trust in your oneness connection.** You comprehend that it's not all about you or all up to you. Life is not about exerting control. You begin to trust the perfect unfolding of your life. You are here to be in connection with others, with the planet, with your higher self, with all that is. All is simply one. You aspire, moment-to-moment, to be a vehicle for light and you take the simple steps that provide "structure" for your light, for your brilliance.

Collective Manifestation Blueprint Exercise:
Inhabiting the New You Check-in

1. Consider how aligned you are to the following statements. You might choose to assign a number on a 1-10 scale. This is not about judging yourself; it's about gauging how far you've come in disengaging from the old paradigm and what further adjustments you might consciously devote yourself to.

Statement	Usually	Sometimes	Rarely
I worry less and less about what other people think about me.			
I don't edit myself (no matter who I'm speaking to) when I discuss my dreams or new visions.			
I tell others about the mystical changes happening in my life.			
I express my emotions freely.			
I'm honest with myself about the habit changes I intend to make.			
I give voice to my authentic needs and desires			
I embrace radical change more than I embrace following societal rules.			
I'm willing to take risks and leaps of faith on my path			
When I learn about the amazing adventures people are engaged in, I rejoice rather than feel envy.			
When I hear about something like crop circles or extraterrestrials, I think, "It's possible."			
I follow intuitive hunches more than I ignore them.			
I listen with an open heart to the dreams and life experiences of others.			
I desire to co-create with others for life experience rather than for ego-fulfillment.			
I sense that it's part of my life path to explore uncharted territory (whatever this means to you).			
I express a pioneer spirit in my life.			
I care deeply for all beings (as holders of divine energy).			

Part II

ESSENTIAL
INTUITIVE BLUEPRINTS

—⟨ઠ૨૨ઠ⟩—

*Hidden within each of us is the soul's abode. It is here
that one's true identity
and creative intention can be surely known."*
~ William Meader, author and teacher of Esoteric Philosophy

Chapter 12

Heart & Soul Central

The only real valuable thing is intuition.
~ Albert Einstein, American physicist

I n this part of *Collective Manifestation* you have the opportunity to learn and play with intuitive processes. These tools will expand your individual consciousness and, practiced together, create more community, group or team cohesiveness.

It can be scary to step out of the confines of mind-based programming — all the ways we are taught how things *must* be and *should* be in order for us to be included, admired and loved. Yet, we are assuredly evolving from the outdated, outward societal model of obey, hear this, do this, don't question, respect, and replicate. We are collectively releasing a black-and-white "be this and not that," standard so that we may inhabit full-spectrum humanness. As intuitive astrologer Sarah Varcas puts it, "not everything in life is about facts. So much of what we need to discuss, debate and consider exists in the grey area of opinion, personal experience and individual perspective."

Human progression is not about a few people being renegades either. It's about everyone waking up to their true human potential and possibility. The wholeness you are being invited to occupy incorporates awakening, acknowledging, listening, asking, resonating, and animating from the inside outwards. If we are to have peaceful societies that function for the many, if we are to create sacred relationships to Earth and nature, if we are to co-create from heart-centered cooperation and collaboration, then we each need to amplify our inner wisdom and bring this infinite resource into play.

The beyond-the-status-quo collective manifestation the world needs will come from inner transformation and the development of inner knowing. When intuition is no longer subdued and ignored it can brilliantly inform outward strategy. Intuition beautifully guides us toward how we best help ourselves, others and the world.

Here are a few of the benefits to developing intuition in service of creating fully alive and optimally functioning communities:

1. Seeing beyond the surface of words, appearances and circumstances.

2. Easier discernment between various options.

3. More apt to receive the learning in all situations.

4. "Down-loading" opportunities and trends in advance of the general populace.

5. Honed ability to piece together puzzle pieces of information and clues because you sense the connection points.

6. When logical paths take you to a dead end, you have a secondary path to information and solutions.

7. More comfort and genius operating outside the status quo, the norm, the usual.

Making the invisible visible

Approach these intuitive processes as the play that they are. They are meant to help take you out of your worrying, doubting, controlling, fearful mind. They are meant to transport you to a realm of magical possibility — which is present when worry, doubt, control, and fear aren't dominating your reality lens. We are socialized to believe that anything worth having is worth working for. Play, we are taught, is for kids. It's something you do as an adult to relieve the tension and stress of work. Forget all that. Collective manifestation is powerful play.

In 2005 I led a dream board workshop for 1,400 people at a personal growth conference. After explaining the process, I had people coming up to me wanting to be sure they understood the directions correctly. One woman had such a panicked look on her face; she didn't want to get it wrong. This really touched my heart, because the truth is that you can't get intuitive play wrong. You are simply making yourself available to intuitive guidance which is always present. The tools are just a means for making yourself available, so intuition becomes noticeable to you. The easier it feels the better (although don't worry if it doesn't always feel easy!). Bring delight, curiosity, and trust along on these intuitive adventures.

Each of the intuitive tools and processes presented here offer creative and fun ways to develop and play with your personal and group intuition. These blueprints can be used to create a more cohesive community through remote, online and live participation amongst groups. The insights you collectively gain expand all members understanding of how they are energetically related to one another. Then community members can better comprehend how they connect to other energetic dynamics like planetary and natural world influences that directly affect what they are trying to bring to fruition.

Through intuition development and higher-self alignment, you can perceive more layers of existence. You can see beneath the surface layer of reality. Such processes make invisible influences and truths visible. You each are able to channel information in your own way (and in multiple ways). You are a permeable being through which knowledge flows. New world co-creators of community are poised to tap into intuitive practices, energy work, and channeling processes light up personal potential and expand global possibilities.

Unified brilliance

Each living being both receives and emits energy in the Oneness Field of creation. We have been trained to filter information through our brains, but receive little training in how to access the wider and deeper well of wisdom available to us through our hearts. Yet, you've all experienced how profoundly your perspective shifts when comprehension drops into the heart. It's that feeling of "I get it" as knowing integrates into your entire system. Sometimes this physically shows up as calm elation, a head-to-toe flush of goosebumps or a tearful expression of relief.

Only through heart intelligence do you move into expressions of compassion, forgiveness, acceptance and kindness. This greatly effects what you then send back out into the world as attitude, gratitude, and action. Living in heart awareness you understand how all choices and actions impact humanity, other living beings and Earth as a whole.

In this Oneness Field, collaboration and cooperation occur multi-dimensionally. One person may explore an area of interest, research an important aspect of your community development, or bring up a question that many are holding without realizing it. At the same time, another group member might investigate a complementary area or aspect and bring this to the group in what feels like synchronicity and perfect timing.

Recently I experienced an entire day of synchronicity. I woke up thinking about contribution and bees. I turned on my computer and there was a campaign for saving the bees, which I contributed to. Later that day I was reading a book with a specific visualization exercise. I smiled to myself, for ten hours earlier I had completed a dream board that was the visual answer to this exercise. And so the entire day went, with me experiencing reality in a hyper sensitive way. It felt both like a demonstration of the perfect timing of each moment, and like a lesson about the illusion of linear time.

Intentional community, whether it joins you with others for a discussion, an event, a process, or puts you in physical proximity for many decades, empowers itself by each member intentionally influencing all levels of reality — those seen and invisible fields. You do this by engaging in multiple realities that rise from different states of being: logical, creative, intuitive, physical, psychological, imaginative, and so forth. Part Two of *Collective Manifestation* presents ways to engage differently, intuitively.

Think of the following three fields as aspects of the Oneness Field. Each field presents ways to put your Higher Self at the helm, to layer life exquisitely. Of course, there is no real separation between these fields; these are merely mental distinctions that may help you practice oneness with All That Is.

Meditation field

Meditation enables you to practice holding space for expanded possibility. In stillness and quiet you create the opportunity for something new to be born. Meditation is a kind of tuning into essential knowing that goes beyond words. Meditation facilitates heart opening in gratitude, joy and peace. Meditation with others empowers tuning into a unified heart-mind. Books abound on different meditation practices. Use our meditative visioning blueprint or find one that resonates with your community development process.

Energy field

In her book, *Beyond The Flower of Life*, spiritual teacher Maureen St. Germain proposes that it is possible to gain access to the energy field through ones senses to the point of experiencing "clairaudience, clairvoyance, clairalience, clairgustance, and clairsentience." It is a journey into the very heart of what is possible for us humans to experience.

In regard to the manifestation of intentional community, begin with heightened awareness of the energy you exchange with others. When you choose to co-create with others you essentially choose to be responsible for the energy you contribute. Mindful of your co-creative energy, you progressively manifest more consciously and intentionally effect collective transformation.

Playing field

Essentially we incarnate to play at what it's like to be human as we play out specific missions and life purposes. We may play at being authentic, play at letting go and forgiving others, play out what it means to live happily, play at connecting to nature, play at expressing parental love, play at tapping into spirit guidance, play at inviting information through astrology and numerology, and play with living forms and design. Of course, there are people who incarnated to play the opposites of these things — such people are what best-selling author and spiritual guide Deepak Chopra refers to as "contrast." As already discussed in Part One of this book, an attitude of play feels essential to a heart-based creation paradigm, as it brings childlike innocence and wonder to the process — an aspect that often gets lost in adult creation models.

All together now

However you want to term it, you are each the master artist, director, writer, designer and architect of your own life and the co-creator of new global community. A heart-based willingness to play with your human life is the best tool you have for creating significant outcomes in the seen world. Here is an opportunity to take all your individual gifts and interests, acquired skills and practical organizational abilities, and combine them with the wisdom of your loving intuition. When each member of community devotes themselves to these aspects, an elegant and effective manifesting force is created.

What I present here are some processes you may use to facilitate energetic, intuitive and creative community development. These will be especially helpful if you have decided to adopt our strategy of creating an energetic foundation as the first phase of your community building.

These blueprints enable you to positively shift and empower your perceptions, beliefs, and vision through shared imagination, sensory experience, and an amplified heart connection to one another and other living beings.

Choose the intuitive tools that resonate with you, and adopt others that work well for your specific type of community and with your service focus. Take the paths of discovery that feel natural for your group. Try processes that take you out of your comfort zone and lead you to new experiences of group potential. Choose tools that bring knowledge and clues to light in a variety of ways. Hold the intention to receive your own insights and guidance and trust that you are always on track. There is no way to get your life wrong. Only you can truly know how to make your life the best expression of your essence. Take a playful attitude and be ready for amazing things to unfold.

Community building is an extraordinary journey. Whatever happens each day is of value. No point in this process is more important than another. It will call for patience, engagement, trust and discernment. What is meant to show up for your community will do so. Your role, like that of the bees, is to engage your life mission, gather resources and to pollinate what matters most to you.

A foundational intuition development tool

Intuitive writing, also known as automatic writing, is a simple way to begin accessing personal wisdom and insights that go beyond the thoughts, memories and information that have been stored in your wonderful brain. It's a way of allowing wisdom to come to you via your heart channel, rather than having to chase information down in a strictly mental way. Intuition can also come through drawing and doodling. Any time you step outside of your habitual thinking-mind you have access to fresh insights and understanding, and you put your most innovative self in charge.

Intuitive writing is an especially good tool when you have specific areas for inquiry and specific questions you would like to ask your guides, your angels, your Higher Self, Source — or however you like to think of the various possible sources for wisdom and guidance. This is a great way to learn to trust in yourself as an innate vehicle for higher wisdom. You are as brilliant as anyone. The truth is that we busy ourselves to block out what we hear both from our dictator brains and from our Higher Selves or spirit. This is your chance to get more familiar with how you receive guidance. Honor what you receive.

Collective Manifestation Blueprint Exercise: Intuitive Writing

Below are two formats that facilitate intuitive writing. Try them both. See if one feels easier for you.

Question and answer format:

1. Begin by taking a few deep breaths focusing on your heart as your reception point.

2. Set the intention that only the most helpful information will rise in your conscious mind.

3. Write down a question you'd like to have answered.

4. Begin writing the response that you sense, see, feel or hear as quickly as possible. Don't pause until you feel the answer is complete. Don't worry about whether or not you are making it up. We make up our lives. We come into this life with a game plan and we have lots of room for improvisation as we go along from day to day — so go with it!

5. Is there a follow-up question that might give you additional clarity? If yes, write the question and proceed with the process again.

6. Review your response(s). Sense into what it tells you. Often, what we receive intuitively has a slightly different tone or phrasing from our day-to-day language. Does it open up a new pathway of inquiry or lead to new thinking around the question?

7. Do this exercise each day for at least two weeks, asking a different question each day. Sample questions:

    *   What are next 5 steps of our community project?

    *   What colors help me to hold a high frequency?

    *   How do I limit myself?

    *   What would empower our group?

    *   What is my inner soundtrack right now?

Writing prompt format:
Below are some writing prompts that will help engage your intuition. It's a great daily practice and an idea generator when you are working with community members on projects. Simply use a prompt that takes discovery in a new direction.

1. Just write the prompt and finish the sentence.

2. Keep writing for ten minutes, without pausing. Let the prompt take you on an unplanned ride. If your mind tries to take over or you feel stuck, just write the prompt once more and keep going. 3. As

you write allow the prompt to loosely direct your energy. Sense the knowing coming into your permeable energy field.

3. Take turns sharing what you have written. You'll learn new things about each other, about current energy dynamics that you share, and about what is possible moving forward.

Sample prompts:

→ I am open to ...
→ If society let go of ... we'd have more room for ...
→ Heaven on earth is...
→ I believe ... is possible
→ We will be living as one world when ...
→ Being inclusive means ....
→ Our best next step is ...

It doesn't matter which intuition tools you end up using. The most important aspect of collective manifestation is that you begin to work more expansively as a group. As Gabriele recently received in a meditation, "Use your collective manifestation power now. Use it in the world. Set your heartfelt intention and focus on one issue or one idea. Concentrate your energy like a laser, like a coherent stream of light and energy at the same time/space, and observe and experience the signposts, shifts and events in the world!"

Chapter 13

Holding Frequency

There's no reference points for new forms we may be creating.
Have to keep going back to the frequency.
~ Wendy Kennedy, "Higher Frequencies" channel

pproach the creation of new community as inner energy expanding outward. This is a significant opportunity to purposefully infuse all that you do individually and as a group with heart. It broadcasts your intent to be authentically seen and known. The inner is reflected in the outer world at all times. The question is what energetic "building" materials have you made available for your community?

As you define and form your communities — where they are located, what they represent, what world issues they address, what human needs they fulfill, what they look like, how they function, and who might inhabit these physical places or online spaces — it is good to keep going back to realign with the intentional core energy you've established. This ensures that the energy you are grounding into the manifested reality, through your ideas, projects, products, services, and communication, is what you intend.

Perhaps your group is meant to generate the energy of deconstruction, irreverence, and non-linear creation. Or you are dedicated to heart-centered kindness, response and service. Embrace the singular essence that you are actively co-creating with your community. At each step renew your intention to fully show up with love, to trust that what you need as creation materials already exists. All you need to do is access what is present in a conscious manner.

Julie Umpleby started Diamond Light World (www.diamondlightworld.net) in 2008 as a way to communicate about how the diamond is the subtle energetic architecture that enables us to connect more fully with our essence — to bridge the world of the mundane with the inspired — by shifting the lens through which we perceive reality. It did not begin as an intentional community, yet has evolved to nurture participants on many levels.

Julie believes that the group dynamic feeds us vibrationally at a different level than we typically experience during our task-driven distracted lives. Her worldwide collective meditations and visioning processes offer people an opportunity to elevate their frequency and envision something different for themselves and their communities. She states, "It's a way of entering into the creative domain of one's real self. It reminds people that there is something beyond the mundane. Shared resonance shows up and through exchanging their experiences people affirm for themselves the viability of this more subtle reality."

Influencing frequency, whether through personal visualization, collective meditations, creativity, prayer, or song, is the invisible foundational part of community building. It's the vital bridge between inspiration and manifestation. Frequency is the portal through which each person learns how to achieve mental, emotional and physical balance. Like others that I spoke with, Julie views communities as vitally important for clarity of self and vision, for the ability to see through illusions and to drop the identities, labels and judgments that limit us in exchange for a sense of freedom and inner calm.

Your inner soundtrack

Holding frequency is not a part time activity. We are always holding and transmitting one frequency or another. At this point in human evolution we are presented with the opportunity to consciously hold the frequency of unconditional love. This is a new beginning for joy and self-acceptance, and we are being invited to regard ourselves as sacred love, the ground through which divinity is expressed. By accepting this invitation, we ready the ground for our new communities which may then be manifested from a frequency of love.

One way to think of frequency is as the inner "tune" one is playing at any given time. It's like when a song pops into your mind and you get the idea that the song is a good indication of your mood, mindset and energy. One morning as I awoke to a beautiful sunrise, the song "Good Morning Starshine," from the musical *Hair*, instantly played on my inner jukebox. It felt like a reminder that we can tune into, or tune out of, various frequencies.

Begin this community journey aspiring to become aligned to the frequency of your Higher Self or your most humanitarian self. Embrace the idea that we are to fully germinate the seed of self-love that is within us at all times. We are the life, the meaning that we seek.

Julie says of the Diamond Light World processes she leads, "As we do these collective processes we're actually inserting future visions, future ideas in to the collective consciousness and breaking down old paradigms. So what is the future we want? It takes divine patience to stay the course and know that we are building new foundations for future people to create from."

The you that progressively germinates self-love, is the self that falls in love with humanity anew and sees others through eyes of tenderness and compassion. You feel your connectedness to your wholeness first then to the greater world. That is how you create new community that mirrors the best of us — by being that which invites the collective sweetness and uniqueness of humanity to show itself. From that heart space you each can more powerfully direct your brilliance with patience, perseverance and passion.

Heart sounding

As my community progressed through intuitive processes explored in this book, the theme of sound, sounding, and sound waves came up in various ways. Sound vibrates, distributing and directing energy in waves. So how might we tune into Higher Self and manifest community through sound? I intuitively asked this question and received the following:

* Tune into heart sounds.

* Be *one* with sound.

* Imagine the sound.

* Be *it* — a sound wave.

* Know that you are heart sounding — each breath is like a wave that goes in and out.

* Surround-sound is the power to vibrate with all things at once — to tune self to all living creatures as you experience oneness (which then gets amplified out into the Universe).

This is not a scientific explanation of harmonics or the role of sound waves. For that you can go online and find detailed explanations. What this does point to is the simple ways in which we can unify our individual heart energy for the good of all — primarily through the simple intention to focus from the heart and on the power of the heartbeat.

According to musician, sound healer and psychotherapist Tom Kenyon, sound and music is the underlying architecture of the universe. Sound allows us to clear emotions, and can link the heart to the brain in the creation of a new universe. In the documentary film *Song of the New Earth* about his remarkable life as a sound receiver and healer, Kenyon applies this idea of co-creating through sound to interpersonal communication, explaining that we co-create the world by how we talk to one another. So using sound to co-create does not have to be a complicated process. We can be mindful of voice tone and the words we choose; these are powerful instruments. (For more information about the power of sound you can begin at Kenyon's website at www.tomkenyon.com.)

There are many ways that sound can show up as a manifestation tool. At one point in my community process I came upon a kind of musical "blueprint" at an art gallery. Even though I did not understand the musical timing notations, the layout of this piece immediately resonated because I had been intuitively drawing a similar shape. It resonated as a way to lay out a physical community, as a kind of sound architecture that could be intentionally woven into our community design.

As part of collective manifestation strive to consciously incorporate the power of sound into your community. This can be done by paying attention to nature sounds and incorporating music into landscape design with chimes and fountains. You might create a sound garden in your neighborhood. My husband's choir group annually sings to the Orca whales that swim in the Puget Sound of the Pacific Northwest. Experiment with a simple instrument like singing bowls and bells. Exchange inspiring music with others on social media. Organize or attend music concerts and chanting opportunities. You might record meditations and visualizations and share them with your group. Start paying attention to your tone of voice when you speak. In my own community, singing shows up often in our meditative visions. We have even received specific musical notes as information.

The overall goal is to optimize harmonious energy exchange in whatever manner comes to your attention and makes you feel joyful. This impacts the world and the universe in unimaginable ways. We can follow the example of others who have responded to the negativity in the world with beautiful sound. As American composer Leonard Bernstein said following the assassination of President John F. Kennedy, Jr., "This will be our reply to violence: to make music more intensely, more beautifully, more devotedly than ever before."

Collective Manifestation Blueprint Exercise: How-to Play with Frequency

There are many ways to hold frequency that helps you tune into your personal intuition and into collective visioning. If you are new to this, start with simply identifying your frequency as "low," "neutral" or "high." Play with tuning your frequency using some of the ideas below. Note what works for you: what easily resonates or lights up your heart. Think of yourself as a sensitive "tuner" or "tuning fork." Begin to make clear choices about what frequency you want to be running through your remarkable heart-centered system.

12 ways to play with frequency:

1. **Tune into sound**. Listen to nature's tunes like waves breaking or bird song and note how you feel. Sing or chant and notice what that does to your energy vibration. Work with singing bowls or musical instruments and notice any changes in your energy or happiness level. Listen to music that elevates your mood.

   Try this: *Hold a desire or goal in your right hand and high frequency (think of a pet, favorite location, whatever lights up your heart) in your left hand. Imagine that your heart is the connection point through which energy flows back and forth from one hand to the other. Feel the energy flow from hand to hand for a couple of minutes.*

2. **Play with color**. Various colors and hue combinations

naturally appeal to us. Notice which ones appeal to you right now. What does that color represent? You might try learning about chakra colors and then visualize them. Imagine yourself immersed in certain colors, the rainbow, or metallic tones. Imagine specific colors or hues flowing through and filling up your bodily system. Note how this makes you feel.

3. **Use scents**. Essential oils and other highly resonant scents naturally elevate mood. Notice how you respond to different scents.

4. **Align to place.** Summon up an image of yourself in your favorite place/landscape in the world. This can instantly transport you to a new frequency.

5. **Light up your heart**. Stimulate your heart center by simply thinking about a beloved pet, or the support you receive from friends and/or spiritual guides.

6. **Respond to form**. Symmetry and geometrical shapes can subtly or powerfully resonate. Try bringing sacred geometry into your community work. How does that simple step affect your frequency? Start noticing all the circles in the world about you. This might help generate a sense of wonder that elevates your frequency.

7. **Enhance your symbolic vocabulary**. The Universe is constantly sending us messages through symbolic language that is present in dreams, dream boards, stories, myths, the animal kingdom, and so forth. Pay attention to the symbols that seem to appear on a regular basis. Pay attention to what symbols you like. Feel into the wisdom of these symbols to appreciate the conversation the world is having with you.

8. **Get your daily elements**. During meditation try holding a crystal, a special rock, or a beautiful semi-precious gem that you love. Does this help you get into meditation or have any effect you notice?

9. **Immerse self in nature**. For some, just being around plants, flowers, and herbs has a calming and nurturing effect. Design your outdoor spaces to uplift your senses and mood. Enjoy diverse landscapes.

10. **Recall resonant memories**. We each have memories that light us up, that feel like special or magical moments. By recalling these we can step back into the frequency tone of that moment.

11. **Move!** Simply stretch, walk, skip, and jump. Any movement will help you to embody and enhance energy flow.

12. **Be more carefree**. Bring more childlike innocence, silliness and joy to your life. We can get caught up in seriousness, control and judgment. Shake off these qualities in favor of lightness, spontaneity, and liberation.

Remember to take a playful approach to exploring frequency. Your desire to be open-heartedly collaborative, fully engaged, and focused on expressing your creative genius will keep you aligned with your intentions for community.

Pay attention to the energy you hold for 24 hours or longer. Then in your journal make notes of the following:

1. When do you sense that your frequency at its highest?

2. What makes it easier for you to hold a desired frequency? And when do you notice going "out of frequency" (discordant)?

3. What seems to be in alignment with this frequency?

4. What are you willing to incorporate into your life to produce a higher frequency: chanting, paying attention to sound during meditation, enjoying nature each day, travel?

5. If the community you envision or belong to could be summed up by a song, what song what would it be?

6. What colors, scents, sounds, tastes, numbers, locations, and so forth, capture the essence of your community's energy frequency?

Dropped energy

Most everyone has experienced the feeling of dropped energy. It's that feeling that nothing is happening with a project or goal, no matter how hard you push. It's your intuition that there is little energy supporting a particular endeavor or relationship. It's the idea that you are not aligned with another individual.

Think of it as a phone call that keeps getting dropped. You take the basic steps to connect your energy and then you pull back emotionally or you get distracted mentally. The result: dropped energy. Perhaps your mind tells you that you *should* do something, yet you are making negative judgments about it. The outcome: dropped energy. When you are not fully invested, but are pretending you are, you create dropped energy.

For instance, recently I applied to be a speaker at an event because I was invited to do so. Yet, I was barely invested in the outcome. Knowing this, feeling this, I should have declined the invitation, rather than create a weak, barely-live connection to this opportunity. I laughed when I wasn't chosen for the event. No surprise. Be fully invested or not. Just choose, be clear, and feel good about your choices.

As you work intuitively with raising your frequency, it's just as important to sense where energy is coalescing and where you have "opted out" energetically, or where you have dropped the energy ball. This gives you a choice to build energy behind a project or to focus on another area with more energy momentum. This means you will no longer pretend that you don't know why something is not working smoothly or manifesting. We like to hide behind "I don't know why," yet this is seldom the case. It's more likely that fear keeps us from wanting to know the truth. That said, there might be instances in which you truly can't sense "what the deal is," yet these will be fewer as you practice tuning into what is present energetically.

At first you can use general identification terms for your project energy status like non-existent, weak, moderate, and strong. As you work with this, try to be more specific. "Weak and fading" is more specific. "Strong and building momentum" is more specific. You might even be able to sense how far the energy around a project extends. Try sensing into the energy range for a project by sensing a status like regional, national or global. Play with the different ways in which you can identify energy presence.

Collective Manifestation Blueprint Exercise: Project Energy Status

1. As a first step list your top projects in your journal or in the chart below. You can even break projects into parts. A book project might have different parts in development at the same time like: research, book cover design, and writing. You can check the status of all parts.

2. Sit quietly for a few minutes, taking a few deep breaths. Think of your first project and ask yourself "what is the energy status of this "name project?" Just sense into what you feel around this particular project. You might hear a word or a phrase pops into your head. If your eyes are closed, you might see visuals.

3. Note the response. Be as specific as you can. In the example I sensed "building" energy.

4. Then if the project needs energetic help, ask what is needed. Note the response. Try not to judge the feedback. Ask for clarification.

Project	Energy Status	Next Step: What is Needed?
Ex: Investments	Building energy	Continue to align values to investments
1.		
2.		
3.		
4.		
5.		
6.		

5. If you sense dropped energy for a group project gather your team or community and ask the following questions:

   ✱ Have we as a community put sufficient heart-centered focus on the project to get it off the ground?

   ✱ At heart do we believe in the project?

   ✱ Have you disconnected your energy from it for any reason? Reaching a dead end with a community goal or project might also occur when you have gotten off track and are no longer aligned with either your core values or stated intentions. As author and Silent Parenting trainer Joyce Anderson says, "Grace is the constant; it's us that keep going in and out of frequency."

It's always better to know the energy status of projects so that course corrections can be made.

6. Choose one of your favorite frequency boosters and apply it to any project you want to keep alive. Maybe injecting energy is a simple case of bringing in another person to focus on the project. Perhaps leadership of the project needs adjustment. Having the group send concentrated heart energy to the project through meditation might help. Projects do not need high energy throughout their lifecycle to succeed. It's natural for energy to flow, to pulse up and down — as long as the connection is there and building in the desired direction.

7. Consider consciously releasing any projects that have become a drag on group energy to the detriment of the outcome you wish to manifest.

8. Check in on the project energy in another week or month (whichever makes more sense given the overall timeframe you are working with).

Chapter 14

Meditative Visioning

We are called to be architects of the future,
not its victims.
~ Buckminister Fuller, futurist, architect, designer, and inventor

Meditative visioning allows you to play with possibility without the limitations you may face in your day-to-day physical world. This is important personal and group development play that expands the energy around what you accept and allow as possible at the heart level.

You are both a receiver and a broadcaster of information. By creating a ritual around intentional receiving, you create an access point that becomes easier and easier for you to step into during meditation. Meditation is a portal to expanded inner vision and to expanded spaciousness. You can think of this access point as a meditation "room" where you meet with others to play with energy.

When I began the New Village 22 community we started with meditative visioning before anything else. We were eager to play with directing our energy through intent and focus. The idea was that by starting with energy play we could experiment with creativity in regard to community development, and experience how this activity/process affected manifestation. We found it to be valuable on more levels than we could have anticipated.

First, the beauty of receiving vision is that with each session you experience being a vehicle for brilliance in a multidimensional manner. You practice having one foot in the energy world, and one foot in what we experience as seen reality. You experience the oneness with which you are a receiver and transmitter of vision simultaneously — you are both the tuning fork that helps to calibrate a new reality and that which is being tuned as a new channel of consciousness.

Secondly, through this process you can hold space for what wants to happen, without an agenda. You can open your hearts to any and all possibility and merely observe what comes into being. We chose this as a primary format because we experience meditation as a bridge to expanded being-ness. The meditation vehicle allows us to better align with what energy wants to come into form. The meditative visioning process seemed like the most obvious way to begin manifesting as a group. Most simply, we chose meditative visioning because it allowed us to begin *being* a community with focus.

This is an opportunity to see what arises as a group dynamic when you consciously engage co-creation differently than you approached it in the past. The main benefits of this process are:

* Learning to play with what it means to hold a frequency and mastering that.

* Anchoring your community in simple love, light and plenty rather than trying to fix the dysfunctional societal systems that exist.

* Entering a field of unlimited possibility. Don't worry about what others consider possible. Agree to hold space for what is possible from your expanded hearts and expanded minds. Allow space for something new to come into being.

* Allowing intention and inspiration to set the energetic starting point for each meditation. Create a playground of creation without worry about "reality."

* Trusting in the power of simple focused energy. No need for mythic pushing of boulders uphill. No more "making" it happen because it appeases the ego mind. The unfolding of new community will come from the connected heart-mind energy of compassion, generosity, inspiration and the simplifying power of humility.

* Practicing non-judgmental creation. Since you have no idea what will rise in this energetic space, don't form mental or emotional attachments to what has to come into form. Stay open to what naturally rises from your intention to create heart-based community.

* Inner vision drives the process. This is not about how "good" you will look to others. It's not about brainstorming ideas. It's about opening your hearts and intuitively allowing spirit to inspire the process.

* Experiencing something you've never experienced before!

The New Village 22 process

Once I had invited the founding members of New Village 22 to join me, the first simple collective decision was to schedule meditations for the new and full moon of each month. We would allow visions to unfold organically. This was to be an inward first process of tuning into what was available for us to know and experience, not a process of imposing an agenda.

We scheduled the first meditation for the November 2012 new moon. At the beginning, our process was to meditate independently at a specific time (taking into consideration our different locations). Later we got more flexible about the time, finding that synchronicities still appeared in our meditations even when we meditated a day or more apart.

I, or another member, provide a meditation "setup" to facilitate a focus that brings us together energetically. This setup is a scene, intention or question that directs our initial entry into our collective meditation space (more on that below). Each person decides how to begin their meditation (e.g., with a prayer for protection during the process, by lighting a candle, or any other ritual they want to establish) and how long their meditation will last. We wrote down what we experienced during the process and shared it with each other. Usually, we will not read the meditation notes of the others until we have completed our own sitting, in order not to be influenced by what they experienced. This makes the process all the more magical for the synchronicities and common threads that appear from this simple practice.

Collective Manifestation Blueprint Exercise: Schedule First Meditation and Complete First Meditation

You may need to consider a few logistics prior to scheduling your first meditation. Do you need to meet with your community group prior to meditation to clarify group basics? Is there a day of the week or a day each month that naturally facilitates an ongoing meditation process?

Your first meditation date or ongoing monthly schedule:

_____

Meditation intention

The first meditation is an opportunity to intentionally hook up your energy with your community partners. Those that have committed to the project each bring a valuable energetic property to this exciting endeavor. By intentionally showing up together, in the same place or remotely from different locations, you establish a kind of energy "room"

154

or space that you will easily enter through intention with each meditation.

The meditation setup and intention will vary and can usually be explained in one or two sentences. You may begin on a boat in a river in one and begin in a desert the next. You may engage in a specific activity in one and request clarity on a specific topic in another. The important point to realize is that your village group or community is a vehicle of love and

Recommendation: *Read the meditation intention and template sections. Complete your meditation **before** you read our "meditation reports," describing our meditation experiences. That way you will come into your own meditation without any preconceived ideas of what has to happen during your process.*

light — a holder for your unique blend of energies. By being mindful of what you have to offer in service of individual evolution, collective evolution, and the healthy evolution of the planet, you direct your vibrational energies with intensity. With this first meditation you are beginning a journey of mastering high energy. Are you ready to play in the energy field?

New Village 22 meditation template

What you are receiving here is a template of how the New Village 22 group proceeded. It is recommended that you use this process as a general guideline, while trusting and honoring what shows up in each meditation for your group. Do not expect to mirror our process.

By engaging in meditative visioning, or any of the other intuitive modalities presented, you will receive steps and ideas that further your energetic exploration, as you establish the foundation for your particular community.

Since we believe that spirit and the world around us communicate through symbols and story rather than language, information about the symbols that came up for us is included for you to consider and understand. You, too, will find this helpful.

Don't worry if you don't perceive the meaning of the symbols that appear for you right away, it takes time to perceive the deeper meaning. At first, just accept the most literal meaning of the symbols you perceive.

This is an adventure. Do not become attached to the need for an "end point." You are engaged in a wondrous process. Find satisfaction and fulfillment in that. You are doing something new. Respect the pioneer part of your being that journeys in a particular direction, and yet does not know exactly what is to be discovered or found.

As you play with this meditation process, research your own areas of community interest and develop clarity about your collective purpose. Trust that ideas for your next meditation starting point will come to you. Don't overthink this aspect. Any starting point for your group is fine. If you arrive at your scheduled meditation without a setup, just start where you left off the last time. You will get where you need to go.

Our meditative visioning experience typically lasted from a few minutes to about 15 minutes. We are constantly amazed at how much can come through in very little time. Determine what works best for your group. For this first meditation I am providing an entire guided meditation to help launch your process. You can record this and listen to it or read it and recall the process.

Sit comfortably with a straight back and feet on the floor. Take three cleansing and relaxing breaths. Quiet your mind. Be relaxed and alert.

Begin by thanking the unseen guides that will accompany you on this journey. Ask for only true and relevant information from the highest path of love and light to come through. Thank your guides for a protected space around you and the other meditation members, and direct all lower energies to be reflected back from whence they came...

Begin envisioning yourself and your group members in boat on a gentle river. It might be a simple canoe or a reed grass boat, or even a glass bottomed boat. Picture the river vehicle that makes you feel contained and safe.

However your boat looks, you're floating smoothly and gently down a river. The sun is shining. The grass along the shore may be fresh and vibrantly green or perhaps it is dry and fragrant. There is a slight breeze blowing the grass. The river current feels friendly, loving, and gentle. This river is sparkling, refreshing, and energizing. Intuitively you and your group bless the river. You feel into the river itself — feeling each water drop that comprises the river. You become one with the water, gently flowing along.

Note where you are sitting in the boat. Where are the other members of your group? Just smile at one another as you connect with your heart energy wordlessly...creating bridges of love between each other... Feel how you are each perfectly placed in the boat for this discovery ride in service to collective manifestation.

Then begin to look about you, investigating the river environment. Note the details of the river and the river bank... Is it a straight river or one with many bends? Are there any stones, branches or logs in the river? Notice without fear or worry if there are potential obstacles along the way. If you sense there are, ask your guides (spirit, animal, angelic) how to best cope with them.

When it feels right, begin to investigate the shoreline. Is there a good place to pull over and get out of the boat? Do you feel inspired to get out the boat or would you like to stay in the boat and go a little further? As you follow your inclination you observe what the other members of the boat are doing.

When you feel that you have completed this first leg of your discovery process, you thank the members of your group on the journey with you. Then you thank the guides that accompanied you.

Open your eyes and gently feel your body in your chair. Take a few minutes to make notes of your meditation experience.

If you are a group that is meditating together exchange impressions with the other group members and discuss similarities and differences. It is not critical that you each have the same visual or sensory experience. Feel the complementary nature of your individual experiences and discuss what it might mean or tell you about your process and group dynamic. If you are a group doing remote meditations, write up your experience and email it to the other members, making notes about any additional thought or comments that rise from the sharing.

Meditation note: It is not unusual for one or more people in a group to feel like they can't meditate. Your mind will try to tell you that you are "making it up." Tiredness and busyness can make you feel blocked from receiving anything. Just keep with it, trusting the process. We found that time after time, regardless of how we felt about the ease or difficulty of getting into meditation, many synchronicities were experienced. Get familiar with the games your mind plays and continue with any practice you have established.

List the main insights that came from your meditation:

*

*

*

*

*

*

*

Significant symbols:

I recommend that you note significant symbols as a way to better understand how the universe communicates to you and to learn the language of your spirit. The universe and spirit speaks in symbol, metaphor, analogy, archetype, myth and story. You can receive this sacred vocabulary through waking consciousness, creativity, sleeping dreams, meditations and other non-verbal processes that open you up to receiving more intuitively. By keeping track of symbols you notice, you will have clearer insight into where you are on your life journey.

It helps to discuss possible meanings of symbols as a group, since this will bring a broader range of knowledge to the process. To glean insight into animal symbols, I recommend reading Ted Andrew's book *Animal Speak*.

List any symbols that you noticed in you meditation:

*

*

*

*

Meditation Practice Recap:

1. Set a date for your first meditation.

2. Set your intention for this first meditation (i.e., to hook up your energies).

3. Try the meditation provided here or make up your own.

4. Ask each person to record their meditative visioning experience.

5. Exchange feedback about each other's experience. For instance, note what is similar and what different information and visuals came through for the members of your group. Note insights.

6. Decide if you want to keep track of symbols and how you would like to centralize this information, such as in a shared document folder stored in the cloud.

7. Discuss any next steps that this experience inspires.

8. Set a date for your next meditation (or a regular schedule like first of the month, new moon or full moon, etc.).

9. Agree upon who will send the next meditation "setup" to the other group members. You can also use any of the ten meditative visioning setups at the end of this chapter.

New Village 22 Meditation:

Below I am sharing the transcript from our first meditation so that you can get an idea about what we received and learned about collective manifestation through this process, and how we reported on our experience. If you find this of interest, additional meditation reports are at the back of the book in Appendix 2.

Melissa meditation report:

The three of us enter the canoe to signify that we are going on this journey together. After traveling just a short distance we get out of the canoe into a field of tall grass. The grass is dry like wheat. We dance, coming together by joining hands — much like a Greek-style dance. Each step feels like joyful permission, like a dance in harmony with nature. It is a blessing bond.

We step in towards the center together with arms raised. We touch hands creating a point (like the tip of the triangle that we represent). We do this several times. Then we bow down moving into the yoga "child's pose" with hands outstretched forward and touching the ground in the center of the circle we've created. Again, we touch hands in the center. We rise facing one another then bend back extending our arms in surrender to the Universe and the greatest good of all. I hear myself saying:

"Blessings, blessings, blessings...
Mother Earth and Sister Sky,
Father Moon and Brother Cosmos,
From you all flows into a creative force of Oneness.
This we pledge, beseeching your assistance
in goodness and grace for our Village Home.
The circle is open! Amen.

Gabriele meditation report:

I see a river with a smooth current, a little simple boat made out of wood is waiting at the shore. Melissa stands in the boat holding a large bar to steer the boat forward. I sit down next to her and close my eyes. The journey begins.

For now all the movement forward is created by Melissa. She is focused on the smooth gentle current and on pushing the boat forward. With my eyes closed I sense the shore. The river feels friendly, with no dangers or obstacles.

With my eyes now open, we see a group of indigenous people standing on the left. Five or six people greet us. They hold decorated spears in their hands; their faces have colored marks. They are welcoming and waving to us, "Hello and many well wishes" on your journey. We look toward them as we pass until we can't see them anymore. I wonder, "How did they know we would come?"

Suddenly the boat starts to float and move forward unassisted. The current has taken on speed and Melissa does not need to push anymore, so she sits down. We turn to each other and put our palms together. It feels like receiving "downloads" from each other, like receiving what needs to be exchanged for now.

It clearly feels like Melissa is the pilot driving and I am the copilot who holds and interprets the map (like in a car race across the desert). The pilot is the one processing this and putting it into action. Now I sense a third person behind us in the middle. This person holds the energy — a very important role! There is also food being prepared or other things done by this person, but the importance of this third person is holding the energy.

Suddenly, a sheriff appears, wearing a cowboy hat. He is in our way and stops us. I wonder, "A sheriff on a river?" But there he is, not sure if he wants to join or to block the way. He says, "I ensure no one takes the land." We reassure him that we don't want to take any land. It feels as if there have been some attempts to take an important piece of land. We reassure him and express that it would be so much easier if we all were on the same side. He turns around and stands in line with us and looks forward with us. I get the sense that Gaia is with us, sending a message that our work is supported, that we should just move forward lovingly and with focus. We should not spend too much time with interferences.

I realize we are on horses now, riding through a desert, we are three plus the sheriff; it feels like we are following him. We ride until we come to a high point from which we can see far into the distance. We stop and look toward the horizon — there is nothing, only sand, blue sky and sun. The sheriff explains that this is "the place" he names it, "The Oasis of Light."

In that moment we hold varying pictures of how the "Oasis of Light" might appear: first as a square city, then like a paradise garden, then like a techno town — it flips in appearance with the thoughts we are holding. Finally I receive the idea: "Gaia has activated, called all her ambassadors."

Paula meditation report:

Clear clean water in the river, lots of tiny fish schooling and playing together; larger fish serenely float by, going about their business. Sparkles are in, above, below and throughout the water drops.

Sometimes the river banks looked blurred and indistinct (just a muddy mess). I got the sense that they need to come into clear sharp relief — that we can't climb out of the water, out of the vision to a place for creating and actualizing, unless we can clearly see the edges of the banks, and see where there are handholds, places to grab onto, and toeholds, too, for climbing up and out of the river onto the land. It's tricky. If the banks are too perfectly in focus, then every stem, every pebble, every tiny grain of dirt is kind of magnified and can draw the eye and mind into its beauty so we get trapped there and stop climbing up and out onto the land and air.

I got the sense that it's best to keep floating and to — this made me laugh — not push the river (reminds of a seminal work in the old consciousness raising movement way back in the days of my youth, *Don't Push the River*). So, I just kind of relaxed into it and let the river flow and take me along with it. The water was so clear and it was easy.

What we noticed and learned about collective manifestation from meditation #1:

After discussion, these are the insights that we received from this meditation.

* We occupy different energetic roles: pilot, co-pilot, energy holder.

* The feeling is upbeat, unrushed, and observational.

* Permission-based rituals help to create a harmonious relationship with all nature on Earth and in the Universe.

* Blessings are an appropriate ritual to open activities.

* Once a project is launched and some initial momentum is put behind it, constant pushing is not necessary when you trust the process.

* It is possible to interact with presences/energies outside the group related to various Earthly issues.

* It's best not to let interference or too narrow a focus create distraction. Keeping a bigger picture view is helpful at this point.

* In the energy realm, it is possible to observe the instantaneous power of thought to shape possible realities.

* Early in the process set the intention for a loving energetic presence in the world.

* Each community is an "oasis of light."

Symbol decoding (full list of our symbols in Appendix 1)

* **River** as life progress (flow), as carrier of energy, as life itself.

* **Sparkles in water drops** indicate presence/atmosphere of expansive energy.

* **Desert** as energetic space between communities, as space for unfolding possibility, as "empty" boundless growth space.

* **Sheriff** as protector-translator of new "laws of the land."

—⦿—

Meditation setups for continuing the meditative visioning practice

If you would like continue your meditation practice using our format, additional meditation setups are provided below. Having meditation setups or entry points to meditation helps you to more easily enter a heart space where your unified energy merges.

Meditation #2: Begin back at the oasis of light — of desert, sand and sky. Join your hearts with bridges of light. Survey your environment. What is present? Imagine a portal being opened for you there. What does it look like? Where does this portal take you? Just follow along with what you see, sense or feel without trying to make anything happen. Also, you might choose to ask your guides what more you can know about each other and your roles in your community creation.

Meditation #3: For your meditation use the following description to begin your energy play, or establish another scene that allows you to join together intentionally.

"Go swimming in the river. Fly in the falls. Wash free from all obstacles and hindrances. Sing like sirens and play. You will meet your helpers in this glade."

Meditation #4: Begin this mediation by imagining that you and your community members are skydiving and landing in the energetic location where you will further explore, enact rituals, and ground your group purpose. If you prefer, you can choose an alternate way to arrive at your location.

Meditation #5: Prior to meditation discuss personal and group intentions that you would like to plant for your community. You may each decide to plant one intention or decide to plant intentions that spontaneously arise in meditation. Decide if you want to set the scene for where the seed planting will take place or if members should let the scene arise organically during meditation.

Sample intentions for the fruition of your community might include:

* *I allow open space in my heart/energy field for fresh visions to seed themselves.*

* *I plant seeds for global plenty.*

* *I intend for wholeness and unity to pollinate among all players who join in this endeavor.*

* *I intend that a strong and lasting energy foundation be established for the easy unfolding of our community.*

Acknowledge that you are not alone in this seed planting — that there are unseen partners now joining you. These seeds will help to focus your personal growth and physical world manifestation.

Meditation #6: Begin by seeing yourself and your group members back at the location where you seeded intentions. Your intention now is to nourish the seeded environment with a flow of your respective energies. This might show up as a kind of baptism ritual, or may show up as watering and tending the environment. Let this flow naturally. Don't try to force what nourishing your intentions has to look like.

Meditation #7: Begin by seeing yourself in a "sound chamber." This might be a futuristic building, a Celtic cave, or an Egyptian tomb. Enter this meditation space and ask to experience what you can know about the importance of sound to manifestation.

Meditation #8: Discuss with your group members where you will meet up. You could choose to see yourselves meeting up somewhere like the Taj Mahal or Stonehenge. It's all play. Experiment with visioning. Use all your senses to help you materialize this place. What is the temperature? What are the scents? What do you see and hear? What can you reach out and touch? Once you enter meditation, see yourself at this location and join with your group members to sit in a circle. See yourselves sharing with each other your wishes for your project. What do you share?

Meditation #9: Set the intention to expand the inner self and your outer space for playing with new possibilities. Start by entering a location you have enjoyed in one of the past meditations. Happily wonder how expansion might show up. Then notice what happens around you or what you feel inclined to do to help with this expansion. What thoughts or visuals do your get? What does this represent?

Meditation #10: Set the intention to hold the highest vision for the formation of your community or group project. Then enter your meditation meeting space and see yourself and the members of your community above Earth. You may be close to Earth or far out into the cosmos. Let this show up naturally. From this perspective experience what it is possible to do or what effect you can have on Earth. Do you have an inclination to go visit the moon? Perhaps you want to visit a particular star constellation? You might want to see yourself as a star radiating heart energy toward Earth.

Chapter 15

Dream Boards

Dreams, imagination, and inspiration are the
beginnings of your co-creative partnership with Spirit.
~ Alan Seale, author of *Soul Mission, Life Vision*

The Universe communicates to you in symbolic language. Likewise your soul connects to you in waking and sleeping states of consciousness through symbols, stories, myths, and archetypes. Through creative awareness you can see your true multidimensional nature, your unique energy blueprint (purpose) and your authentic soul essence (symbolic energy you). This awareness enables you to tap deeper into the multidimensional being of light that you are.

Dream board creation allows you to begin identify personal symbols that are the language of your soul. You step out of your logical, language-based mind and into creative visual-based consciousness. It's a way to gain instant updates about what you are mentally, emotionally and spiritually processing. Through this intuitive, non-linear, no-agenda process, meaningful messages from one's higher self are communicated. Each intuitive collage holds multiple levels of meaning. You learn to access wisdom directly and in layers, rather than looking outside yourself for your best answers. If your intention is to be your best self, then developing intuitive abilities is essential.

I have been creating intuitive collages for more than fifteen years and teaching this process since 2006. My attraction to collage is three-fold: it's creative, it's informative, and it's mystical. From the moment I realized that my collages held clear messages for me — that they were speaking to me — I acquired the ability to witness my personal and spiritual unfolding as it was happening.

This intuitive process gives anyone the ability to access information about what is happening energetically, and what is on the verge of physical manifestation. It's a way of creating intentional space for what wants to show up. You get a deeper, wiser perspective on yourself and how manifestation works.

Of course, creative processes have been used for decades as a team building exercise. Dream boards are ideal for developing intuitive ability while examining the qualities you want to foster in your group. Through the deconstructive nature of collages you can play with breaking apart what is known to create something entirely new and surprising.

For instance, by deconstructing existing photographs of architecture, nature and so forth, you can envision into possible new building forms. It doesn't have to make sense to your brain. You don't have to play according to what's possible in the physical realm right now. You can go beyond all boundaries and construct as the spirit moves you. That's how you begin to manifest beyond imagination.

The dream board process blueprint (for individuals or groups):

1. Choose one magazine (trust that the universe always provides what you need).

2. Move though the magazine quickly, being alert to visuals that catch your attention or light you up. Tear visuals out without worrying about what they mean.

3. Begin collage composition on a piece of paper you have chosen (size is up to you). Feel into which visuals want to come together. Don't force anything. You probably won't use all the visuals you tore out.

4. Cut visuals as inspired.

5. Glue visuals down in any way you choose. Composition may change from initial layout as you glue. Keep your "judging" mind out of the process. There is no way to get this process wrong, just as you cannot get life wrong. This is creative unfolding.

Tips for decoding your intuitive dream board

* As you look at your finished dream board, quickly give it a title.

* Let your left brain tell you a story about what you have pictured. If you feel that your dream board has a "beginning" point (top, bottom, right, left, center), start there and quickly go through the story aloud. Make notes.

* Ask your intuition what certain pictures represent. Trust what comes to mind and write it down. This helps you understand your soul "vocabulary" that comes through symbols, story, geometric patterns, and color.

* Notice if there's an overall theme. Themes like connection, love, beauty, crossing new thresholds, transformation or relaxation may be revealed.

> **TIP:** *As with all intuitive dream boards, you can't mess up its creation or take away the wrong message. However you see it, and whatever you perceive, is right for you. Accept that it is a perfect reflection of your energy at this moment.*

✳ Pay attention to picture arrangement. Is there a key central visual from which others radiate outward? Does the layout move from right to left or from top to bottom?

✳ Ponder the significance of overlapping or neighboring pictures. Is there a connection? Is there a mini-message contained in the connected visuals?

✳ Stand back from your dream board and look at it from across the room. Do you see new patterns or shapes? What does this perspective add to your understanding of the dream board meaning or messages?

✳ What is the dominant color palette? What does this convey to you?

✳ Are there any words pictured? What do they communicate? (core values, priorities, qualities to invite into life, areas for energy expansion?)

✳ Keep your dream board where you can see it. Naturally multi-layered, additional meanings will reveal themselves as you are ready to receive them. We tend to need processing time before each new insight or revelation appears. An open, curious perspective is best.

✳ Take a step(s) to honor what your dream board shows you. The more you do this, the more life clues you will receive.

The universe is, at all times, trying to support your goals, dreams and soul evolution. Through awareness and intuitive creativity you can begin to better notice the sacred sign posts presented to you each day.

Think of dream boards as a portal to expanding your spiritual or intuitive vocabulary.

It's important that you take a step or steps that honor what you see on your dream board. If you receive the message of relaxation, integrate some form of relation into your day. If you receive a visual message to take a leap of faith, take the leap that is right in front of you. Is it a physical, mental, or emotional leap? Typically, once the visuals are in front of you, you will easily see what you are called to do or be.

Perceiving layers of information

Dream board layouts often show layers of information. These layers of information can be presented horizontally like layers of a cake (from top to bottom or bottom to top), or vertically like slices or film frames (right to left or left to right). A dream board may feature a central visual with "spokes" of visuals radiating from it or may feature an unfolding spiral layout.

Linear layers might hint at physical process steps lining up, or emotional and spiritual alignment. Linear layers might show your energetic frequency or vibration. Dominant color themes like black and white might be conveying information about polar opposites being side by side or blue and white might indicate that a new "blueprint" of some kind is entering the picture of your life. The Collective Manifestation Energetic Cycle Chart in Chapter 18 can also provide visual clues that will help you with decoding your dream board.

I perceived the following manifestation information that came from a vertically-layered dream board. The stacked-up layers were quite clear, so I approached decoding by looking at each layer.

First Bottom Layer: The PREP stage of manifestation. This is where the props, accessories and tools of future manifestation are gathered. Here the clear intentions (pictures of fruit seeds) and the projects (pictures of eggs) we wish to birth are stacked up. Of course, because we are always bringing something to fruition/manifestation at all times, projects that have "ripened" (pictures of ripened fruit) come into physical manifestation at the same time as we start new projects/dreams/intentions.

Second Layer: The PRE-PARTY stage of manifestation. Pictured was an elegantly dressed woman surveying beautifully laid tables. It reminded me of that moment of calm before a dinner party, when you can appreciate all the work you've put into preparing something wonderful that others can enjoy. This preparation stage was visually the meatiest layer of the dream board. Here the stage was set for success by lining up all the energetic and physical materials needed. The message I got was that at this point in the manifestation process we have taken actual organizational steps that are in flow with our vision. It's a good time to pause and appreciate what we have accomplished thus far.

Third Layer: The PARTY unfolds stage of manifestation. Here the realization of our vision and dreams begins to unfold (dinner party underway). At this stage we are out in the world with poise and confidence, which is pictured by a famous and respected woman who is waving at the viewer. As our authentic self we are friendly and comfortable with who we are authentically — we own our brilliance (starry sky over woman). As our dreams unfold and come into being, we share the wealth (dinner abundance) of what we bring to the world. We celebrate with others what we have manifested.

Forth Layer: The GIVING-BACK stage of manifestation. Heart-centered manifestation is the energetic offspring that we present to the world and to the universe (picture of the world in a nest next to a picture of the cosmos). Here we receive abundance (pictured as a lovely blooming garden) and give back (words "art of giving") from our completed projects and dreams.

As you can see, taking one element, like the layout, can greatly facilitate the understanding of messages that are present in the visual design.

Combining intuitive processes for dream board decoding

Intuitive practices can be used together in dream board decoding for remarkable results. For instance automatic writing is a great way to decode a dream board. Here is an example of an intuitive question and answer format that enabled me to get at the heart of a dream board. I simply selected different collage elements to ask my intuition about.

Q: What I am seeing in this dream board
A: Vortex momentum.
Q: Who is the hang glider?
A: Higher Self
Q: Who is on the wind surfing board?
A: Optimal Activity Self
Q: Who is the woman cut out like a windsailing board?
A: The Reflective Self that guides "the trust."
Q: Who are the people positioned inside the lit-up bowl?
A: Your energy-stream. It will take a village to keep up momentum.
Q: Who else is pictured here?
A: Your team, your angels, and yourself as you are now and always.
Q: What do the legs and feet represent?
A: The status of your process and next steps.
Q: What is the "winged" building structure symbolic for?
A: What it takes to get lift: the team, your Higher Self, your optimal action self, the energy behind the seen, the grace of God.
Q: What more can I know about this dream board?
A: All is being birthed in the ocean of spirit divine. All is delivered from beyond the physical world. All drops in to show up as manifestation in the streaming flow of life.

Dream board decoding can both reflect how you approach understanding your own life and it can expand the meaning you find in different life elements and events. Hopefully, it helps you to take a more playful approach to manifestation. Remember, there is no way to get your life wrong. It's all just unfolding that leads you to the next intention, choice and step. You are constantly layering your life. Don't like something? Layer it with something new. As a group or community that co-creates, this viewpoint can help you to stay flexible and not take it too seriously.

Collective Manifestation Dream Board Exercise:
What Is Our Group Manifesting?

Creating a group dream board can easily help to direct the group's intentions, focus and efforts. Intuitive projects like this can be used to keep a group's efforts on track. You can intuit the need for change, the emergence of new opportunities, and recognize shifts in group energy. You can see:

* Where your community is in the conscious manifestation cycle.

* What is lining up or needs to be lined up.

* Qualities that will facilitate easy manifestation.

* The energy dynamics you are currently playing with.

* Insights into what is happening at the invisible energy level.

1. Create a dream board using the blueprint instructions as you hold the intention to more clearly understand what you are currently manifesting. Options for this are:

   * One person can take on this creative endeavor on behalf of the group with members providing their insights about what the dream board is revealing to them.

   * You can gather together live to create one or more dream boards (perhaps you want to set different intentions for each one).

✳ Work independently and then meet on SKYPE or via Google Hangout to discuss what is being revealed or shown in each of the dream boards. If you want to do this as part of a conference call, simply exchange photographs of each other's dream boards ahead of time so everyone can reference the various dream boards.

2. Discuss the dream board.

3. Agree on at least one step to take based on the information you receive.

Chapter 16

Accessing the Akashic

If we could first know where we are...
we could better judge what to do, and how to do it.
~ Abraham Lincoln, American president

The Akashic Records is a kind of cosmic information field or library holding information about the journey of your soul (past, present and future). It is collective spiritual consciousness and is also referred to as The Book of Life. By intentionally accessing your records you can get direct answers to questions about your life path purpose, what you may know about current global circumstances, and how you can best facilitate the unfolding of your group or community intentions.

The Akashic Records is a portal to expanded knowing. It's a way, too, to align your spiritual path with your community effort. You can even access the Akashic Records of your community, for it has its own recorded spiritual consciousness.

As Akashic Records expert Linda Howe explains on her website, www.akashicstudies.com, "The Record is an experiential body of wisdom, insight, guidance, and healing information. It can be accessed by means of a simple sacred prayer. Saying this prayer causes a shift in the consciousness of the reader sufficient to register the subtle impressions of the Record. It is a mutual action, where the reader moves into alignment with the Record — and at the same time, the Record moves within the reach of the individual reader."

Much like intuitive writing, accessing the Akashic Records occurs via a question-answer format that enables you to tap into knowing beyond what the brain stores as knowledge. The process involves opening a session, asking questions in a specific manner, and then closing the "reading" session. An expert resource is Maureen St. Germain who offers live and tele-courses on this practice at www.maureenstgermain.com. A highly accessible book on this practice, *How to Read the Akashic Records: Accessing the Archive of the Soul and Its Journey* by Linda Howe. I highly recommend both.

Now is the time to become your own life guru and expert. Seek your own wisdom first, before looking outside yourself for additional resources. When you do so, the complementary information you need will appear more easily in your awareness. The more ways that you can learn to access your highest heart wisdom the simpler it will be to fulfill your aspirations and to have a profound effect for good in the world.

Below is a sample reading that I did for New Village 22. The tone of voice and language here is specific to me. It is typical for the voice to be different from your everyday tone and language. As you learn to read the Akashic, stay open to how information is delivered in terms of words and phrasing. It is a bit like learning a foreign language. Sometime you might be unsure of the exact meaning of words. I often ask for additional information for more clarity. Trust that you receive knowing in many ways. Your everyday personality is but one filter for bringing understanding, and learning into your life.

Sample Akashic Records reading:

Q: The full moon is tomorrow. What is the next step at the energetic level for the village?

A: "Now is the time for all good men to come to the aid of their country," pops into my mind. This is a phrase that I learned in typing class, so I relate it to writing. Also heard the phrase, "Bring in the architects."

Q: Who are the architects?

A: Your mind self, your creative self, your beingness, your spirit self.

Q: Is there a physical action step I can take to move New Village 22 into realization?

A: Be at one with All That Is

Q: What is the best way to be at the "drawing board" for New Village 22?

A: You are it. You are the drawing board. It is not an action. It is beingness. Hold vibrational frequency now and forever.

Q: How do I hold vibration for the physical location of New Village 22?

A: I see a wave moving over land. I am picturing energy waves and structures rising up. Miracle structures, too, that have never been imagined before. What is new, what is possible by the open hearts of many. Then I hear, "Be that which you want to be at all ages, in all times." I see the members of New Village 22 sending out waves from our palms. We send out waves of healing for the release of shame, fear, victimhood, friendlessness, anger. We send out healing waves with the thought "may all be cleared in the bay of love and hope. We are sending these waves up to an "intensifier." Like a big square board on a tall pole (like a stadium light pole). The waves bounce off this apparatus and go out into the world.

Q: How will I prepare?

A: You will tune into possibility. You will connect your communication genius to a transmitter of good news and tidings. You will share the plenty of New Village 22 in terms of: goods, new inventions, thinking, creative theory and play, experience of this place, Oneness wonderland, paths of glory.

Q: What are the paths of glory?

A: Oneness in intent. Oneness in prayer. Oneness of heart strings. Oneness of action. Oneness in sharing. Oneness in birthing new. Oneness in honoring all.

Q: What is Oneness of intent?

A: Same path. Same goals. Chosen path. Laid down vibration. Tuned frequency. Established time-place. Work outside linear limitations. Call into being from trust and faith and focus on what can *be* in this world, this universe, this cosmos beyond all memory of time and space. Beyond, beyond, back to pure nothingness when all existence was one grain of sand. One point of perfect silence.

Q: What is Oneness in prayer?

A: After intent comes focus. Focus brings the energy into a kind of living prayer, where all is sacred living. Nothing is apart from its sacred nature. Discount nothing — mostly yourself. Hold all to be in alignment with peace.

Q: What is Oneness of heart strings?

A: Love, happiness, song, play, kindness, consideration, compassion, simplicity.

Q: What may I know about Oneness in action?

A: There will be a time for this step and it will flow incredibly easily and well from paths before it. Come in peace to serve all paths; build momentum from this. Keep releasing anger, shame, fear, victimhood, less than feelings for self and world planet.

Q: What else may I know about New Village 22?

A: The song "Somewhere" from the play-movie *Westside Story* pops into my consciousness with slightly altered words, feeling like a message about a new world, new communities, and new ways of living on Earth in the future.

This reading once again affirmed the importance of approaching community development and participation from the intention to be unified and whole, and to stay focused on expanding from the heart-center. From a focus of serving the paths of all beings, all is possible, and all that no longer serves is released. Manifestation then becomes the result of energy flow throughout a highly dynamic system of both seen and unseen forces.

Chapter 17

Eartheart Matters Process

All truths are easy to understand once they are discovered;
the point is to discover them.
~ Galileo Galilei, Italian astronomer and scientist

T he Eartheart Matters process created by New Village 22 community member Gabriele Neumann is based on traditional constellation work. Constellation work is a therapeutic systemic
modality founded by German psychotherapist Dr. Bert Hellinger that
attempts to discover and heal multi-generation family dynamics and
longstanding issues. Constellation work is ideal for helping individual community members to clear personal issues that block full open-
hearted participation in group projects.

Groups, teams, and systems of any kind, can adapt the constellation
work format to more clearly see collective energy dynamics — that relate to internal relationships, relationships to nature and spirit of place,
as well as relationships to the greater world and All That Is.

Typically, the Eartheart Matters process begins with the "client"
(individual, business or community) identifying an issue that needs
resolution by asking a specific question or setting a clear intention to
gain insight into the matter. Gabriele then occupies each of the main

positions that play a part in the dynamic being observed and healed. She intuitively receives information as movement, emotion, or words from the "knowing field."

Example of Eartheart Matters Process

Gabriele decided to use her Eartheart Matters process (an adaptation of constellation work) as a way of checking in with the energy of New Village 22. We regard New Village 22 as developing its own essence and spirit, as being a living entity in the unseen realm of energy, as we hold frequency for its ongoing manifestation in the unseen realm of initial creation. Below is her report.

I begin by asking the "spirit of the village" for the best intention for this work and receive that the relevant question is: "What needs to heal/happen so that New Village 22 benefits in most beneficial ways from the energetic information of the lunar eclipse?"

I move on to listing the participants/positions for the constellation system I will be working with. I write each on separate pieces of paper and intuitively lay them out on the floor. This allows me to step into each position and receive the dialogue, feelings and gestures that are being communicated to me from the different "perspectives."

Participants/positions:

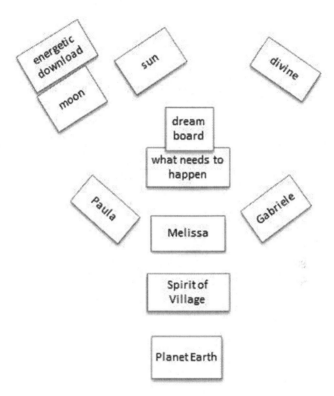

* Planet Earth

* Sun

* Moon

* Energetic Downloads now available through Lunar Eclipse

* Spirit of New Village 22

* Truth of New Village 22 (added later in process)

* Divine

* Melissa

* Paula

* Gabriele

* What Needs to Happen so that New Village 22 benefits most from the energetic downloads available now? (Here I got the impulse to add Melissa's first dream board for the Lunar Eclipse on a separate paper, printed in greyscale.)

The following describes what I experienced as I occupied each position and the participants interacted.

First Phase: Perceptions in Starting Positions

Planet Earth
Furrows its brow, eyes are closed. Stands upright but head is towards the ground, and says twice: "Not here yet, not here yet."

Spirit of the Village
Feels very airy-fairy beautiful, like the young woman I had seen in meditation, wearing a floating white dress. She dances gracefully, acknowledging every position in the system, but she does not feel firmly connected to anything.

Moon/Sun (put together to connect to the Lunar Eclipse)
Eyes closed, I receive the words, "We have already moved on in the dance of cosmic constellations."

Moon

Eyes open, facing the system. Looking at Spirit of the Village the Moon says: "Always shading my wisdom over the Village." My arms circle upwards, creating an overlap (intersection) in the middle.

Sun

With eyes open and a straight posture, the Sun speaks to the Spirit of the Village: "I am the father of this cosmic child. It is on my beams that energetic information travels. Don't obstruct this process of love and light." I gesture to indicate connecting Energetic Downloads to Spirit of the Village. I feel that the information does not flow freely through these positions yet. I observe that What Needs to Happen and our team members are in-between these positions.

Divine

Arms open wide and eyes are looking at the constellation system (the combination of all positions). Very awake and lovingly addresses the system saying: "This is so great!" Simultaneously I feel a massive love-wash running through my body, bringing tears up. I receive the words, "You are so blessed, this is so beautiful, there is so much love for you!" Divine feels like it is embracing the whole system.

Melissa

Eyes are closed and standing with a straight balanced posture. Smiling, hands are on stomach. Feeling is that the "Spirit of the Village" and "Planet Earth" are behind her. She says: "That is my baby, absolutely my baby."

Paula

Eyes are open. The feeling is happy and balanced. In the position of Paula I look at everybody/everything in the system, acknowledging all that is there. A feeling of knowingness pervades and she says: "I am absolutely right here, this is absolutely right."

Gabriele

Eyes are open and I face the whole system. I feel like weaving all the parts together. My arms start an unfamiliar dance, like a dancer who uses very particular arm and hand gestures to symbolize specific meanings. I dance around What Needs to Happen and then move around all the other participants. This lasts for about 2 minutes.

What Needs to Happen

Eyes are closed with hands in front of face. I hear myself saying: "It feels so heavy, so heavy." With these words I sense the greyscale dream board picture positioned next to me.

Energetic Downloads

Immediately I receive the words: "I need to pass through" and look to What Needs to Happen. I use my arms and hands to show how I want to get through to the Spirit of the Village.

Second Phase: The Constellation Process Work begins

What Needs to Happen

Says now: "What Needs to Happen is an alignment with the Truth of the Village.

I get the impulse to print a color version of Melissa's dream board and to add "Truth of the Village" on it and to put this next to What Needs to Happen. Remove the greyscale copy.

Truth of the Village

Says: "My truth is all your authenticity, all your love, all your potential, all your compassion and all your well-being."

What Needs to Happen

I ask: "What needs to happen for New Village 22 to benefit most from the energetic downloads available now?"

Answer: We need to move out of the way.

Question: To move out of the way, what does that mean?

Answer: Move yourself out of the way. Ground yourselves so that the nodes can be set.

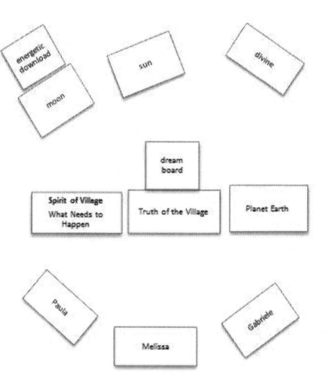

At this point in the process I feel the impulse to reposition the constellation system participants. Spirit of the Village is layered atop What

Needs to Happen and joins Planet Earth in the middle of the system, alongside Truth of the Village, with the color print of Melissa's dream board. They are positioned in front of Paula, Melissa and Gabriele. I feel like placing a lit candle floating in a bowl of water on Spirit of the Village and do so.

Spirit of the Village
Now says, "This feels like the most gracious birthing channel." Smiles and is very happy, very grateful.

Planet Earth
Says, "Now I get the connection. Don't know how, when, where, but I do feel and get the connection now."

Energetic Downloads
Now happy, says twice: "Getting out of the shadow into the light." My hands are directing a flow of energy toward the system. Then I receive the words, "You three are holding this baby in your divine womb. You carry it out." Again great love washes through my body. With my inner vision I see that there is no need for protection, that all is well at all times. By feeling grounded and authentic our community grows.

Final Phase: Concluding perceptions, feelings, and insights arising from shift in relationships between positions/participants

Moon
Smiles, with arms open toward the system, saying, "Always shading my wisdom and love."

Sun
No words, yet I feel the exchange/transmission of information in lightning fast circuits.

Spirit of the Village

Says smiling, "Such a graceful resting point, like being rocked in the womb." *Analog sign: I notice that at this stage my water candle floating in the little bowl stops burning, the water has reached the flame.*

Truth of the Village

Says, "I am like amniotic fluid, the nutrition in which the baby grows."

Planet Earth

Says, "I feel so honored to receive this baby." A huge emotional wave of sudden understanding comes with the words, "I am the mother." Planet Earth speaks very lovingly, full of emotion, to the Spirit of the Village: "Oh my dearest child, my dearest child."

Gabriele

Says, "This feels very beautiful; I am honored to be part of this. This is what I truly want to do." I have tears in my eyes and truly and deeply feel that this is the work I really want to do.

Paula

Thought appears, "Like above, so below, like above so below." Looking very lovingly and full of knowingness toward all the participants of the system, feels even more happy now, feels rightly aligned.

Melissa

Speaks aloud, "This change feels so good," indicating with hand motions the transition from protecting the Spirit of the Village to opening up toward the system participants to receive and exchange information and downloads. It feels very different, like holding a bowl being filled up with the Truth of the Village.

Energetic Downloads
Says, "How do we feel now? Full of color, explosions of color, fireworks of color!"

Divine
Feels very satisfied, and says: "A true birthing channel and path for growth and expansion. All is well."

What Needs to Happen
Says, "Alignment with truth has happened."

This Eartheart Matters process enabled us to appreciate all the energetic relationship dynamics at play in our community building process that were beyond our mental radar. Through this process we learned what needed to happen so that the beneficial energies of a lunar eclipse could positively affect the whole system. We needed to ground ourselves, and consciously shift our "making it happen" vibrations so that energetic downloads of the eclipse could align with the heart and truth of the village. It also showed us how the simple steps we took in the physical world and through our intentions had profound reverberations in the energy world and in our community process. As a result, we more clearly understood our ability to be in alignment with cosmic forces, and the importance of getting out of our own way in order to manifest in alignment with more expansive wisdom.

According to Gabriele, like other systemic and intuitive processes, the Eartheart Matters process contributes to the lifting of personal and global consciousness by directly accessing and working with the "compassionate heart" of groups/teams/whole systems. "Through a deeper understanding of the energy dynamics at work, all concerned get a broader view of the blockages that created the situation and how resolution and new divine balance can be attained. This view into, and acceptance of, 'what is' allows for deep transformation and healing on the soul level. From shifts in perspective coherent heart solutions and better decisions come forth, allowing all to meet life with greater love, well-being, kindness and compassion."

This process is a true healing modality for collective manifestation. It allows for questions to be addressed in a different manner, for new solutions to appear, and for the energetic symmetry to become visible. This process can be applied to:

* Understand and heal family concerns and lineage patterns.

* Understand and heal group, community or teamwork related concerns.

* Make an energetic evaluation of a project and how it will unfold.

* Address personal questions like "Would I benefit by experiencing life in a community abroad?"

* Become aware of all the energy dynamics affecting the productivity and success of a business or community endeavor.

* Gather information about leading a group or community around a specific topic or global issue.

* Real estate and property issues like identifying the right place to live and finding co-community members for an investment property.

* Specific design and land use questions like, "Does this forest agree to our community development of tree houses?"

It's not unusual after a constellation process for intriguing incidents to happen. As Gabriele says, "Things happen in magical and synchronistic ways to show us that our energetic being and our physically manifested life are always connected. There is a deep communion between all in life."

Part III

MANIFESTING COLLECTIVE BRILLIANCE

—⚬⚬⚬—

*Life is not what you alone make it. Life is
the input of everyone who touched your life
and every experience that entered it.
We are all part of one another.*
~ Yuri Kochiyama, civil rights activist

Chapter 18

Magical Realism

Now is the time to understand more so that we may fear less.
~ Marie Curie, Nobel-prize winning physicist and chemist

P art One of this book presented foundational core ideas and
practical organizing exercises for creating intentional community. Part Two presented intuitive tools and energetic processes
that layer your heart-centered intentions with a boost of soul guidance.
You've explored how play and intention creates space for a more open
global mind, and how collective healing and frequency coherency generates a more open global heart. Now we'll look at how these multidimensional layers bring about the manifestation of magical realism.

Community as signature energy

The spirit of your community will be imbued with its own personality. Your group will naturally have a unique energy thumbprint. It's like
a song or piece of art that is instantly recognizable as being by a particular artist. Another way to think of this is that the energetic essence of
your community is like a fragrance distilled from particular aromatic
compounds. For example, New Village 22 is enlivened by a signature
energy blend of friendship, audacity, and possibility.

The energetic essence of friendship is a vibration of delightful companionship. It is a loving and supportive vibration. We willingly engage together and each bring our own unique mind-heart-soul potency to this essence. This is the energy of invigorating alliances. There is an easy rapport of give and take at its core. We are thankful for the friendship extended by all our unseen guides that help us along this path. All we nurture on behalf of New Village 22 is created in the spirit of living more consciously connected as friends.

New Village 22 thrives on the energetic essence of audacity. As Paula humorously says, "We are willing to be the wacko out front." Audacity is daring that eschews the conventional. We foster an environment that can absorb the unusual viewpoint and the unexplainable. We consciously break from limiting social programming in order to be more adventurous and to consider new options. We aren't constrained by tradition, nor are we out to flaunt it. It's just not an interesting focus. What may appear bold to others is really just a fun and exciting way to approach change and to accelerate self-development and self-expression. Audacity makes us feel alive; it gives us courage to speak our truth and to live authentically. From this audacity we report on our experience so others may be inspired to generate their own unique signature energy and perfect process.

We mindfully incubate the energy of possibility. This vibration of openness is expressed in our willingness to envision and to hold space for fresh unfolding. We come to this life experiment with no agendas or a fixed plan for how it will all turn out. This means befriending the unknown. We accept and welcome the shifting nature of life in these fascinating times. We daily exchange wonder, beauty, and the surprising. This energy sparks ideas and our collective imagination. The energy radiates readiness, enthusiasm and playfulness. If we assigned a visual symbol to this essence it would be fireworks that express our bursting optimism, expanding intuition, brilliant connections, and whole heartedness.

The blend of these signature energies are what you will recognize in New Village 22. It's our hope that should you interact with us, or come upon our community in the future you will think, "What a friendly, creatively irreverent place where potential flourishes."

Collective Manifestation Blueprint Exercise:
Define the Spirit of Your Community

So what is the essential energy or spirit of your group or community? What energetic presence do you wish to occupy in the world?

1. Defining the spirit of your community can begin as a discussion about what energy lies beneath your intentions for community. What is the spirit, the energetic juice that will enliven these intentions?

2. Try making a list of adjectives that conjure your essence. Then distill it down to three to five qualities. Which ones stand out as the high notes of the energy blend that is your signature?

3. Discuss how this essence is expressed through your group, organization or community.

Alternative exercises:

A. You may define spirit through an intuitive writing practice completed individually and then shared for refinement. Simply have each member begin with the prompt: "The spirit of our community is ..." or "The essential energetic qualities of our community are ..." Continue writing for a minimum of five minutes and a maximum of 15 minutes. Intend to keep writing without interruption. If you feel your mind start to take over the process, simply write the prompt again and continue.

B. This is the perfect exercise for creative play, too. Create a dream board or try any other intuitive creative practice that allows you to capture the essence your unique collective energy.

Noticing energetic power alignments

Community building and creativity often moves in waves. As you continue to explore and expand your own intuitive processes, you will increasingly become aware of what is present to work with. Keep connecting the dots of what comes into your awareness in terms of people connections, resources, information, and fascinating areas for exploration. The layered clues and meanings are always being revealed to you. You notice them when you are ready to move to the next step of your community growth, and when you are ready to integrate the wisdom these clues lead you to.

Additionally, you will perceive the multi-layered dynamics present in your community experiences. Liliane Mavridara is an author, poet and thought leader who synthesizes her European descent with her eclectic professional background in business, psychology, personal development, holistic health, media and the creative arts. More than anyone I know, she knows how to become aware of what is available to work with in various communities and how to intentionally let those communities shape her heart-centered engagement and contribution.

Since 1997, Liliane has been actively exploring various world communities, from Glasgow and London to San Jose and New York City, helping creative people to own who they are and what they want to do. She helps them, as well as herself, to manifest harmoniously for the good of their community and the greater world. She does this by allowing herself to be an outsider who knows how to become an insider. She intuits what locations will facilitate her personal and professional growth. She becomes part of communities with the intention that they be changed for her presence and knowledge, although how that happens often takes her by surprise. "There's always a reason I go to a new place, and usually things change to make the experience different from how I thought it would be," Liliane says. "Yet, opportunities arise that I wouldn't have encountered had I not taken the leap." Intuition plays a big part in her choices about where to move and who she will align with. Then she researches the dynamics of the community to ground her intuition into a more practical application of service to others. As she says, "What I bring to community is a different perspective that facilitates openings. I create bridges so the community gets to the next level, whatever that is."

Collective manifestation energetic cycle chart

From our own research, meditations, and creative intuition tools the New Village 22 group has perceived alignments between particular energy frequency, symbols, and manifestation dynamics. These alignments signal specific opportunities (doorways) that help us to mindfully evolve our collective manifestation.

What the chart below shows is that in the beginning of our meditative process we found ourselves visioning a desert location. This felt aligned with being called to open our minds and to allow emptiness, while detaching from old ways of approaching our lives. The shifting sands of this symbolic desert location signaled change. At the same time, big open landscapes were showing up on dream boards — a kind of message to make room for the new.

As we proceeded, I kept track of the energetic cycles we experienced through all the blueprint practices I share in this book. There was ongoing discussion about how we perceived the information we received through practical awareness and our intuitive exploration. I decided to chart the information to provide us with clarity about the layered experiences.

Keep in mind that you are always at different stages of manifestation for various life aspects. You may be at one stage regarding a relationship, and at a different stage in regards to a job, a location move, or a specific project, and so forth. The first column is the signature essence of the energy. The second column notes how this energy may show up to you symbolically. The third column describes the main dynamics of this energy, and the fourth column the key opportunity for consciousness expansion being offered. I have added some ideas about how you might honor this energy through physical action. The fifth column notes how you might step into this energy flow. You can begin at any point since time is not really linear, and you may have a preference for beginning your community journey aligned to a specific energy other than fire.

Use the *Collective Manifestation Energetic Cycle Chart* to help you understand what phase of manifestation you are currently experiencing, as an individual and in regards to your community projects and intentions. Pay attention to what is popping up in your daily awareness. Notice what is coming through your meditations and creative endeavors. You are being asked to mindfully occupy all the moments of your life, so that you are conscious of what you are manifesting. When you do so, you will notice how quickly you manifest.

Collective Manifestation Energetic Cycle Chart

Elemental Energy	Symbolic Locations	Dynamics at Play	Key Opportunity and Invitation	Collective Manifestation Phases
Fire	Desert Volcano Fire pit camp fire	Emptiness, openness, New possibilities, space for new knowing and passion to enter. Creating consecrated ground. Expansive Sun energy.	**Change/Activation Portal** Wear colors like red, orange, yellow; light candles during meditation or place candles on an altar; visualize dropping limits into fire.	**Initiate** community based on inclusive Ideals, heart inspiration, intuitive impulses, and a desire to contribute. Release limits and blocks.
Earth	Fields Underground	Grounding ideas, seed planting, egg hatching, fertility, animal guides. Ritual and procedural frequency or energy.	**Reception Portal** Gather tree seed pods/acorns; grow or create meals with seeded fruits and vegetables; plant seeds, use orbs for rituals.	**Set intentions** and define scope of group or project. Each member commits to devoting skills, talents, gifts.
Metal	City Above ground	Grid, supporting beams, "bones," geometric structure and energetic network. Conducts, supports and facilitates expression of creativity, change and transformational frequencies.	**Heart-Creation Portal** Wear gold, silver, copper jewelry; use architectural tools to imagine new forms; play with holding the frequency of sacred geometric structures.	**Discern and create** energy form, steps, projects and technological paths. Empower individuals through supportive connections. Provide structures/avenues that allow collective energy to unfold and show up.
Water	Beach Sound Pool	Nurturing, momentum building, frequency conduction, washing away unhelpful energy, baptizing the new, crystalline structure. Moon frequency.	**Transition Portal** Drink plenty of water; take detoxing baths with sea salts; use water features for interiors/exteriors.	**Focus** on the flow of plans and projects. Where is there resistance and where is flow easy? Enhance connections and communication at all levels. Release limits.
Wood	Forest Glade	Germination, assured core growth of each being, unity of sacred connections. Where incoming and outgoing meet. Conscious & intuitive energy.	**Integration Portal** Create rituals using wood bowls or musical instruments; plant a tree; honor what trees contribute to planet; pay attention to posture.	**Build up** core energies. Connect all that feeds your confidence. Direct heart-centered energy into new development for all. Feel secure about what has come into being as the result of your attention and nurturing.
Floral	Countryside	Blooming and opening. Active manifestation. Intention and focus lead to effective action. Expansive, celebratory energy.	**Flourishing Portal** Enjoy flowers in the garden or home; use floral essential oils and ingestible flower essences. Enjoy color in art, clothes and nature.	**New realizations** showing up as blooming energy. Material outcomes appearing. Results from leaps of faith that fully engaged your true powers.
Air	Mountains	Maturation, new level of insights and mental understanding. Connection of heaven and earth. Spontaneity. Angelic and universal	**Evolution/Movement Portal** Use breath exercises, singing, chanting, speaking from highest self; engage movement to embody new	**Attain** big picture view of progress and contribution. Higher-self perspective of next steps/opportunities.

These alignments are not linear. They are related layers (so nothing is really ever missing). Each portal presents an opportunity to consciously step into the manifestation process, and two or more layers may be occurring at the same time. For instance, you may notice both symbols of metal and floral energy, perhaps pointing to the need to create structures for the growth that has occurred. Symbolic fire and water energy may indicate that a balancing or emotional release is transpiring.

This Collective Manifestation Energetic Cycle can be used to track any community focus from health to technology development. The terminology might be changed to reflect your specific focus and the key points of progress. I encourage you to create your own chart to identify important process markers, informational connections, and the symbols that make sense to you and your group. You will experience similar alignments that bring deeper meaning to what you are trying to accomplish and that significantly nurture your community development process. You'll begin to really appreciate that indeed your heart-based efforts are having a ripple effect.

There is an organizational elegance to this collective manifestation cycle that begins in emptiness and openness, and progresses through to a cosmically charged place of radical creation. With intention, focus, and emotional resonance, desirable manifestation can flow easily and be experienced as magical.

Chapter 19

Light Into Form

Participation — that's what's gonna save the human race.
~ Pete Seeger, American folk singer-songwriter and activist

O ne of the remarkable aspects of the New Village 22 project is
that holding oneness of vision has been the easiest thing imag-
inable. Perhaps it is because we are meant to work together
in this co-creation. Maybe it is an outcome of being willing to suspend
ego-mind expectations or agendas about how this is going to turn out.

The single most dominant message we received during our initial meditations and intuitive practices is that it is time for humans to
evolve by playing as the unified Oneness that we are.

We need all the innovation, invention, and creativity humanity can
produce. We need heart-and-soul driven projects led by caring people
who have a vision of the difference they can make in the world. It's the
creative and out-of-the-box vehicles and projects that will give intentional manifestation a powerful way to show up.

As Millennial commentator and blogger Pippa Biddle sees it, hard
core challenges are coming up for her generation in next 25, 50, 100
years that require that the status quo be challenged and that people challenge each other. She explains, "We're only able to face those challenges

if we get the best minds working on them and they are connecting to each other, and if they feel welcome to question the way things work. One person is never the solution. It's about the community. Only way we get there is if we engage."

Whether you gather in the same room or a virtual room, each person is part of the solution of how to support others in open-hearted ways as well as how to ask for support in manifesting one's own vision.

Creating forces of change

Community building and growth at this time in our human history is a fascinating process. We are operating within a shifting world dynamic that can feel chaotic. That's the exterior truth we deal with. The interior truth is that by choosing to intentionally work with the energy field, you can expect to feel both unanchored and excited about new creation possibilities. It helps to accept that you are working with the unfixed nature of possibility. It's like newly seeing the world through a microscope. What once seemed solid (daily life, relationships, career, health, and financial status) now feels like buzzing elements seeking resonance and taking new form.

Embracing possibility requires embracing fluidity. Everything is in the process of becoming.

Keep going back to your intentions, your core values, your practical skills and your intuitive understanding of what is needed. This will serve you well when you become fully engaged in community.

In her experience working abroad as a teenage volunteer, Pippa found that her intention to create good was not enough. "It was too vague. I needed other skills that would enable me to do what I truly intended." She tells the story of how she and other "voluntourists" were in Tanzania to help build a library. Each day they would lay bricks in their novice-like way, and each evening the local workers would have to undo and redo the work, never saying a thing to the volunteers about it. When she volunteered in the Dominican Republic she realized she couldn't help the way she intended because she couldn't speak the language proficiently. Ultimately, she realized it was better to lead from her best skills — skills like speaking, connecting with young students, and working with teachers about how to use curriculum. She also points out that "a big thing for young people is realizing what their skills are. You have to help them find them and build on their skills."

As an initiator, who quickly learns the lessons of her life, Pippa made the bold decision not to complete college. At twenty-one she is the chief community officer and director of talent for BrightCo, where she manages a community of young experts, connecting them with companies that want to be aligned with young people, technology, and social good. She also serves as a youth representative to the United Nations for The Jane Goodall Institute. As she says of her drive and the Millennial world view, "We expect different things than previous generations. I ask questions in my writing and speaking, rather than give answers. I like taking systems apart (like our voting system) and seeing how they can be reworked. I am constantly questioning protocols and pushing myself."

Effective collective manifestation is about knowing what each person is good at and how to apply various skills. Also, it's becoming aware of about what you need to learn in order for your actions to align with your heart intentions.

Keep making space for what wants to show up easily through your group efforts. Keep making adjustments based on new understanding and new opportunities. Continue to let yourselves be surprised. Build trust that your new community makes a difference and that each step is an "energetic" accomplishment that contributes positively to our shifting world.

Most importantly, don't be deterred by naysayers. Albert Einstein famously pointed out, "Challenges to new ways of being in existence are always challenged by the status quo." As more communities emerge to challenge social stagnancy, new vision, values, and lifestyle elements will be integrated into the heart of the global community. In fact, it may happen sooner than any of us can imagine.

Individually, and as a group, don't be surprised to keep experiencing what it means to be brought into balance. For instance, one week I might feel confident, like I can access the answers to anything, and the next week I get a humbling life lesson about understanding that I have no answers for anyone, that each person makes their own choices and comes to their own answers in their personal perfect timing.

The oneness group dynamic works best when you seek to inspire, support and help shift energy in each other, while all the while knowing that it's both a personal and collective dance. As Raja Choudhury says of the benefit of hosting a social media group the size of a small town, "I trust the advice of about 20 to 30 members in my virtual community more than I trust the advice from people in my 'real' life. The people that stay long, participate most, share and counsel most, form a core group, which one could see as a collective guiding force and a wisdom force in its own way. I see this emerging all the time and I love it."

Going to your various communities for support is a vital part of creating a one world community. Through all phases of manifestation it's natural to flow between a full spectrum of feelings and realizations. The Oneness Field holds it all. Nothing is extraneous; every stage of physical development, emotional growth cycle, and each moment of spiritual enlightenment belongs.

Transformation of the world dynamic is both a privilege to take part in and, at times, an overwhelming endeavor. It requires the suspension of all our old mental programs like worry and the need to control the outcome. We are here to be channels of loving creativity. It's not about "What is the best thing I can think up? It's about "What is the best I can expedite from the heart?

You will capture what is possible through the particularities of your community. No drama is necessary when choices are made from the heart. Right action is discerned honestly. At each stage receive clarity about how to seed intention, perceive from awareness, expand your beneficial presence and direct your energies from the heart without fanfare.

When inner and outer reality are one

While writing this book and pondering the process of how you manifest anything, I was lucky enough to sit at a window with an expansive ocean view. This provided the sense of no barriers between me and the outer world, yet I was comfortable and safe. This perhaps is what we long to experience in community — the feeling of contributing to big picture evolution, while feeling secure within a communal framework of being seen authentically.

Heart-centered manifestation has begun to feel like there is hardly any separation between intentional energy and visibly manifested form. It's merely a habit of mind to believe you're miles from the finish line or your dreams are out of reach. Like the tides coming in and going out, manifesting energy is always present. Energy is always transitioning into a visible effect or outcome.

We have been socialized in the West to focus on final material form — the carrot that dangles in front of us. Yet, all stages of manifestation are worthy, valuable, and rich, like the sacred cycle of sunrise, high noon and sunset. Just as we would never expect to experience a sunset all day long (well, maybe in some very northern locations), we waste our precious energy by not engaging the potential of all the moments in front of us. This is another good reason to begin community play in the energy field. It is an opportunity to learn patience, and to appreciate unexpected experiences of wonder and magic. It's a chance to enjoy the full-range experience of manifestation.

Giving form to your light

Central to creating a heart-based community is the awareness at each step that what you are really doing is giving physical form to love and light. The heart is the tuning fork that helps you to tune love into each step. The heart is the connection point where vision meets the urge to act. The heart is also your integration point for all that you release outward and for all that you bring inward.

Throughout our own New Village 22 community development, we have remained open to what unfolds. Starting as a remote energetic community, we have directed our vision inward to more fully observe the process of creation, while we gathered clues from the outer world that were in alignment with our community pillars.

From this experience we have found that:

* From collective willingness → we breathe life into community oneness.

* From the spark of intention → we create process that takes us from "I" to "We."

* From release and surrender → we clear the ground for healing, balancing and new multidimensional experience.

* From the joy of creativity → we offer the vehicles of our individual gifts/strengths to the exploration of collective possibility.

* From enthusiastic learning → we connect the dots of understanding and bring substance to our vision.

* From conscious being → we connect to and nurture a multitude of opportunities that arise organically from a balance of mental and intuitive heart brilliance.

* From the desire for authenticity → we produce transparency of expression and build trust.

* From the space of expanded vision → we transform ourselves and the world.

By understanding and using the dynamics of receiving and giving simultaneously, collective manifestation begins to feel more organic. Each group and community will have its own way of living into its vision for the world, of materializing remarkable expressions of love. You can't go wrong. Your group, team or community can't fail. It's all play; it's all discovery; it's all invention; it is all sacred. Each change-minded community makes a difference.

For instance, by being a leading voice in social media, Suzette Sommer, and others like her, highlight courageous and inspirational people around the world who are helping others, and connect those people who might benefit from knowing what each other is doing. By shining a light on social, cultural, environmental, and political areas that present huge opportunities for innovation and change, awareness and understanding flourish. In this way the social-media community fills the huge gap left by what traditional media doesn't cover. "We are the editors who decide what the world needs to know about. We add information, fact check, provide context and historical perspective, says Suzette. "We do this together, not in a vacuum. Every day I see some good result that social media has brought about by simply putting attention on some issue or situation. Social media gives humanity an effective voice." That's powerful collective manifestation.

Raja Choudhury believes that we've just scratched the surface of what is possible when humans interact and collaborate to expand cloud consciousness. "Conscious community has not intersected well with the gaming community, but it's coming," Raja says. He's currently working on his Universal Quest concept. "We're working on ideas about how you can map your own online quest and invite others into this reality. You might say, 'I want to take a global tour of high energy places or places where Earth meridians are powerful and where I will feel awakened.' I'm interested in developing a questing tool that you can share with others so all users have input about what is experienced and what they get out of it."

The benefits of creating communities, online and off, is unlimited. As Raja says, "You never know what wisdom will come, what ideas will emerge, what new thoughts may just change your life, what people suddenly show signs of enlightenment — it is quite wonderful to see enlightenment and spiritual companionship evolve in unusual ways amongst members." Have no doubt. The community wave is building, and it is propelling connected individuals and forward in the expression of heart-centered ideas, intentions and positive effects.

Chapter 20

Living as a Heart Force

Making the simple complicated is commonplace;
making the complicated simple, awesomely simple, that's creativity.
~Charles Mingus, American jazz bassist, composer and bandleader

T o live as community is to be that which you envision. *Be* the village that you already are. You are its heart, its cells, its arteries, its organs. You are the model of divine love the world looks to for inspiration and uplift. Look about you and identify all the signs of loving co-creation around the globe. Whether you envision creating community events, belonging to an online community, coming together with others for specific business projects, or would like to establish community at a physical location, celebrate all who are already making their heart-centered presence known, and are already a unified force of love.

As Megan Gaiser passionately says, "It's time to collectively raise our leadership standards, starting with each one of us. We get to choose what types of leaders we will be. The result of that choice shapes what kind of world we will create."

Consciously continue with the dissolution of dysfunctional social programming and activate new social structures in keeping with your hopes for change and progress. Tune inward and outward as the receptive beings you are and continue to integrate the sacred heart-wisdom you receive into your intentional community. Make leaps of creative expression, using the best of what is coming from unlimited hearts and minds. Take a stand; use your voice to connect to others. Ignite personal and collective passion that stuns the world with its soulful kindness and innovative magnificence.

In the end, this desire for more functional and loving community is perhaps a pathway to perceiving our neighbors, our friends, our project participants, our colleagues, our creativity supporters, and our innovation funders as one community. The World Wide Web has already created the foundation work of creating a structure that gives us the sense of being one global community. Now we are expanding this informational platform into physical reality. We are connecting our knowledge with our inner wisdom, and giving form to new paradigms.

This transition point we occupy is critical. In the past predators, war, competition, societal drama, and world tensions drove community together for survival, security, and for a sense of belonging to the "right" clan. Now the threads of creative possibility, cooperation, consciousness, healing and love are weaving new community together for a greater sense of inner and outer wholeness. As this first book in the *Collective Manifestation* series has explored, love-powered intention is the activating force behind the co-creation of a joyful, healed, abundant and more peaceful world.

11 Collective Manifestation Keys

As you have been exploring throughout this book, collective manifestation is an ideal playing field for awakened consciousness. More than ever, each of us can sense where we are going and why. We can, layer by layer, experience life multi-dimensionally in a fulfilling manner. We find the deeper meanings and insights along our collective paths. We choose to intentionally join our energy with others to produce something more powerful, and with more ripple effects in the world and beyond, than ever before. At every bend in the river, there is new possibility being seeded. Celebrate that nurtured collective dreams are taking root and will continue to flourish in amazing ways.

Understanding the keys to collective manifestation helps to empower your role as a change pioneer. Using these keys will help your group to intentionally be a dynamic influence for good, and to be a unified force for miraculous transformation in the world.

The 11 Keys to Collective Manifestation are:

1. **Identify portals of opportunity.** There are portals or access points for working with energy. For instance, identifying the meditative visioning process as our primary vehicle of discovery was such a portal. Attitude and intention is a portal. Change is a portal. Creativity is a portal. Time is a portal (as we experienced by working with the moon cycles, eclipses, and equinoxes). Different group formats are portals. What is the group activity that generates cohesiveness as it allows you to establish an energetic "room" to work in? How can you explore, discover and innovative in outlandish, remarkable and even quirky ways? These portals will free your process.

2. **Occupy simplified inner space.** Create sacred inner space in your life for something new to arise and take form. Release ego-mind control and set the intention to let soul drive. Let go of old patterns and habits as you heal issues of your first tribe (your family), as this clears energetic space for new roots and growth. At every bend in the road, consciously bring grace into your community process by releasing control of what the outcome must look like. As you continue to do the deep inner clearing work individually, you empower group consciousness and become a more unified and powerful vessel through which global community shines.

3. **Plant clear vision and intentions.** Fortify inspired and unified vision with heart-centered intention. These intentions provide coherence for the unfolding of collective manifestation. From the force of collective heart know what you're purposefully calling into being. From what collective energy signature will you bring manifestation into form? What difference will this make to the world?

4. **Tune into opportunities to be creative.** Take a broad perspective of creativity. Creativity is taking an out-of-the-box approach to solutions. Creativity is allowing personal growth to present new opportunities for transformation. Creativity is shifting focus and trying new paths to success. Creativity is combining skills and talents playfully to offer something entirely new in order to help others. Individually and collectively tune into the opportunities that are presented easily to you. We're socialized to overthink. Focus from the heart. Creatively develop projects that are a good fit to your community vision.

5. **Hold steady collective love frequency.** Recognize how individual vibrations work together like the different colors in a rainbow. The power of the group comes from each individual knowing how to connect to their loving self that needs nothing AND that is enlivened by the immense creative potential in front of them. When group members run different tracks of worry and concern (personal drama) the collective frequency dips back into the denser vibration of ego mind. As a group run uplifting tracks of optimism and inspiration. Holding love frequency also means mastering the idea of holding opposites at the same time (think of a piano keyboard with both white and black keys). The fewer judgments any one person makes about the specific "key" that has to be played, the more "compositions" you have to play with as a group. One person may be holding the frequency of divine feminine while another is holding the frequency of divine masculine in order to create complementary

energy. Honor these differences. As you discover what makes your community hum, you will generate more love frequency consistency, and power up your community to its fullest expression in the world. You will realize that holding love frequency *is* the ultimate manifestation.

6. **Find effective vehicles for your collective light.** This means using your talents, skills and interests to create effective applications for your community's collective brilliance. This may be events/conferences, products, services, creative projects within and outside your community, technical inventions, scientific innovations, healing modalities, or activism for important change and social justice. Choose a centralized activity that unifies your group, while providing enough independence for members to explore additional outlets for their gifts, skills and genius. The main point is to make the shift from an attitude of "what will I get out of this?" to a conscious attitude of "what do we have to contribute?"

7. **Germinate wholeness.** Processes at the individual level are indicative of what is moving through the collective as a whole. Individual growth sparks collective progress. Diversity is important to the long-term health of the whole. Continue to develop your whole-self aspects: your full powers of presence and process, leadership and humility, cooperation and initiative, abundance and generosity, gentleness and fierceness. Community is ideally adept at seeding and birthing, at dreaming and acting. Also, continue to germinate (e.g., bring the fire of your passion to) the structures with energetic foundations under them (the projects/plans you seeded through intention and have nurtured with focus). These will be effective transport systems for your collective heart mind.

8. **Align with your Higher Self perspective.** This is typically the big-picture view, the more expansive perspective of a situation.

Unlike the mental mind that wants to draw conclusions or declare the ending to a situation, the Higher Self aligns with divine grace. Only then does possibility expand far beyond mental outcomes. The Higher Self knows how to allow true power to surface. The Higher Self has access to many layers of meaning and understanding. Higher Self perspectives easily intuit what is best for all concerned, not in a patriarchal manner, but in an inclusive and balanced manner.

9. **Play in the seen and unseen**. The more your group or community appreciates the power of having one foot in the energy realm of fluid possibility and one foot in manifested reality, the greater the collective force of your intention, focus and action. Why not get the best of both worlds? The more you engage intuitively, the more you will get comfortable with the true potential of your co-creator role. Seek to understand change dynamics (personal/collective) and to how to stay open for what wants to unfold. Inspire individuals to connect their own vision for personal fulfillment to inclusive community vision. Treat all aspects of creation (seen and unseen) as equally vital and real. You are being gifted with an expanded manifestation playing field. You are ready to play here.

10. **BE ALL IN as ONE Force**! Be passionate. Take leaps of faith. Withhold none of your brilliance. Be whole hearted. Focus on the quality of your relationships and practice connecting to the heart of all Earth beings. Respect each facet of your collective brilliance and be integrated as one force. It's not that you stop being an individual; it's that now you choose to play with what's possible when collective energy acts cohesively.

11. **Celebrate each cycle of expansion.** Celebrate how the development of your community empowers all. Celebrate being a positive force and presence in the world. Celebrate creation and how it makes everything possible. There is no better manifestation fertilizer than

the energy of continued wonder and inspired enthusiasm. Let celebration support your vision for creating a more glorious world.

At each stage of collective manifestation pose questions, review what has transpired, receive feedback and keep all lines of communication open. This is critical to evolved communities that are able to walk their talk and keep to the path of the heart.

Collective manifestation guiding principles

As you experience and play with the collective manifestation keys stay aware of some simple guiding principles. These principles came to our awareness through all the processes described in this book. While there is much more we can understand about these principles and this is not a complete list, it is possible to facilitate manifestation by layering in these principles. Do so as you are inspired and are presented with opportunities.

Related to individual and collective heart energy:

* Making a leap into the unknown can be joyful and playful when you are inspired by heart intention.

* Take a "hands on" approach to directing energy (both in the energy field and in physical reality).

* Remember the importance of energy in and energy out. Creation is a heart energy exchange, it is not one-sided.

* Form flows from alignment of discipline and joy.

* Focus on group heart unity (hold steady to uplifting intention) so as not to get pulled off your center by individual concerns and worries.

* The heart is the best guide and compass.

* Heart frequency/vibration is the most important construction material of new community.

* Holding high frequency for 2 minutes a day for 45 days will help bring form to community.

* Create energetic heart bridges (connections) to members of your community.

* *Now* is always a good time to seed heart-centered intention.

* You need to nurture seeds of intention with heart energy.

* Balancing and integrating opposite qualities is essential to keeping heart centered.

* Your heart is *the* connector; the primary manifesting portal.

Related to collective power (community frequency):

* The more people involved in community, the more "pollination" occurs.

* Awakened consciousness is the core of world transformation.

* Awakened consciousness bears new gifts.

* At the energy stage it is possible to raise structures and to play with changing the "building material" through thought.

* Members of the collective create structural integrity by believing in the group effort.

* Community diversity (of thinking and so forth) is important.

* Applying the skills and talents of each member is vital.

* At all stages community is already complete.

* The collective is meant to be a grander force than the individual. Do not stay stuck in beliefs about what "I" can do. Grow into belief about what "we" can do together.

Related to clearing energy:

* Focus on clearing personal blockages and issues to be a more efficient vehicle for intentional community manifestation.

* It's vital to release old issues while holding one's ground (focusing on heart frequency).

* Remove old inner walls (of limiting beliefs, resistance to change, etc.) to make energetic room for the collective to play.

* Release what is not needed. Release anger, shame, fear, victimhood, "less than" feelings related to Self and Earth.

* You cannot clear another's personal wounds without permission.

* Healing rituals are helpful.

✳ Never hold onto energy; let it flow.

✳ Hold the vibration of love to clear fear and the need to force things to happen. This invites in grace and miracles.

Related to creation/creativity:

✳ Use imagination and visioning to move creation beyond the norm, the status quo.

✳ Drama (ego mind driving life creation) is no longer the dominant propelling force of the collective.

✳ Divine heart-mind energy is propelling human progress.

✳ Tap into the freedom and joy inherent in the creation process.

✳ Ideas initiate manifestation. Ideas summon coalescing energy that then builds into various levels of form.

✳ All aspects of your whole Self contribute to creation.

✳ Infusing creation with qualities like peace, joy, and excitement will make a difference in your creation being positively received by others.

✳ Seeding intentions is critical to new creation.

✳ Many seeds are sent out from divine as inspiration. This leads to manifestation themes appearing around the globe and being anchored into the collective consciousness by multiple sources.

✳ How people work with intention varies. Some people will plant seeds of intention in a direct manner. Others might hold seeds of intention in reserve until it feels right to focus on these seeds.

✳ Magical realism aptly describes the multidimensional process of manifestation.

Related to nature:

✳ Asking nature for permission to interact with it can take place through energy processes (guided meditations, energy healing, etc.), sacred rituals, and through direct relationship.

✳ An open and trusting heart easily aligns with the environment.

✳ Plugging into nature allows groups/communities to recharge with ease.

✳ Earth is propelled by the invisible forces of One.

Related to sound:

✳ To tune into waves of sound, tune into your heart.

✳ Paying attention to one's inner sound track helps manage frequency.

✳ Singing, chanting, sounding and so forth helps to keep the collective heart centered.

✳ Chanting OM and other sounding actions help bring energetic forms into being.

* Sound and color are heart energy conductors.

* Energetic structures can be tuned. Personal frequency is the tuning fork.

* Collective heart songs play out into world/cosmos at all times.

Related to spirit:

* We are supported by and connected to our spiritual lineage.

* Prayer and blessings facilitate energy building.

* New communities can energetically connect to supportive beings.

* The Spirit of each community is a spiritual teacher.

* Oneness is the path of glory.

* Asking for sacred support and assistance is critical.

* Energetic rituals acknowledge the creation of sacred space.

Related to energetic structural qualities:

* The diamond carries the essence of the new world.

* The integration of divine feminine and divine masculine energies fosters balanced manifestation.

* Directions and Elements combine as creative forces.

✳ Various Self aspects are the "architects" that help build and root energy structures.

✳ Sacred geometry is important.

✳ There is new DNA to work with.

✳ Each community member energetically performs an important task or activity.

✳ It is helpful to identify specific frequencies that aid community creation or development. This may be an affinity for a specific location or particular color frequencies, and so forth.

✳ Embrace the process of form in transition. Prior to physical form possibilities remain open.

Your world mirror

In the old paradigm, it was the mirror on the wall that held the prevailing power to assert your value. In the new paradigm, you choose to honor your value by applying your gifts and talents in the way that most interests you, that most brings you joy. Your connection to others and to all beings is your source of manifesting power.

What is in your heart as loving vision, inspiration, intuition, passion, care, and generosity will progressively show up in a unified world community as ideas and innovation, form and structure. It may not happen overnight, but already collective energy has galvanized, and empowered attitudes, beliefs, and relationships are manifesting a new reality. It appears as sustainable buildings, equalitarian societies, interaction between disparate disciplines, innovative economies, creative explosions of sound and color, respectful interaction with nature, and joyful movement. Keep a happy focus on this magical display.

As leadership trainer Suzanne Anderson so beautifully put it, "There's something in the 'we' space between people. When it's consciously opened up then there is something that happens that increases the force of the whole. What downloads in the space is a kind of fresh wisdom and love. Something that happens that isn't available until you come into the geometry of community."

Epilogue

A Love Letter

Gone are the days of guarantees, but the days of opportunity?
They are alive and well.
~ Pippa Biddle, Millennial writer and blogger

Dear Visionaries of Heart-Centered Community, there have long been visionaries imagining ideal community. Such visionaries have considered why community should function differently and who might occupy such a community. These visionaries have proposed diverse scenarios about what architectural forms would facilitate function, how society can more effectively impact the happiness of its populace, what technology developments would enhance human abilities, how to co-exist more harmoniously with the environment, and what significant contributions to the evolution of humankind such a community might foster. You join this community of visionaries as the leaders, co-creators, teachers, and healers.

Visionaries of the last fifty years have had varying degrees of success creating intentional communities, communes, ecovillages, co-housing developments, and utopian landscapes. Yet, regardless of so-called success in the implementation of their visions, these creators' focused energy and clear intention has shifted the collective mind and imagination. They paved the way to progress by passing along their ideas about community potential that can now be translated into whatever form you choose. Here is just a small sampling of visionaries, and their manifested communities or conceptual societies, that you might find inspiring and fascinating to know more about:

* Falco, born Oberto Airaudi, (Damanhur® Federation of Spiritual Communities)

* Eileen Caddy, Peter Caddy, Dorothy Maclean, (Findhorn Ecovillage)

* Swami Kriyananda, born J. Donald Walters, (Ananda Village)

* Mirra Alfassa (Auroville)

* Paolo Soleri, (Arcosanti)

* Jacque Fresco, Roxanne Meadows (The Venus Project)

* Buckminster Fuller (Cloud Nine)

* Starhawk and 14 person Creation Team (O.U.R. Ecovillage)

You are the pioneers manifesting new reality now in innovative ways both imagined by such visionaries and in phenomenally creative ways that couldn't have been conceived before now. At this point in our human history, the size and scope of community matters not. Visionaries around the globe are working their magic in their specific expertise for the good of their communities in areas like architecture, sustainable design, ecology, art, agriculture, energy generation, education, alternative health, permaculture, personal growth, and spirituality. Networks of intentional online communities connect global participants in a single "room." There are cloud communities where technological inventions are being actively supported. These are the new hives pollinating fresh possibilities.

What matters most is your intent to amplify the energy of love. What matters is the opening of a heart space where positive contribution, exciting and useful exchange, and the nurturing of possibility can take place. What matters is each of you taking steps toward the realization of your dream. Remember, it's all just play. If you haven't already, choose to be part of a community that is connecting heart energy around the globe through exuberant and diverse engagement.

> **Love Blessing**
> *All is beauty and blessings.*
> *All is peace and prosperity.*
> *All is coming and going.*
> *All is flow.*
> *All is one.*
> *Be this.*
> *Love the life that you are.*

Without ever having all gathered in the same room, we at New Village 22 fully consider ourselves to be community. Already we support one another. Already we daily unite our sacred energy in the creation of what we are uniquely able to envision, hold space for, and bring into being. Already we contribute the harmonious energy that we generate and expand through our processes and projects. The discoveries continue to flow as I prepare this book for publication. We have gained a fourth member and have completed more than 40 meditations. Our relationship to our guides is strong and we continue to be amazed by the synchronicities and magic we experience.

We are eagerly engaged now in the design phase of intentional community building and look forward to sharing that fascinating process with you in *Book Two: Creation*. It will feature interviews with community leaders about what works and what doesn't, as well as exercises for designing all aspects of community, and a range of possible group projects that you can make your own as you continue to engage the collective manifestation process.

Book Three: Action will focus processes and tips for bringing your community to life with grace, gratitude and love. We'll also share the surprising manifestation stories from others who have embarked on this journey.

We are but one face of new community, and we hope to connect to the many remarkable communities that are taking root and flourishing. You are not alone, your community is not fighting against a tide of negativity; rather it is contributing to a growing surge of heart power manifesting magnificence everywhere. As the newest member of New Village 22, Barbara Krauss says, "We are the carriers of the seeds, and the givers of birth. We are the holders of the light, and those who willingly and lovingly construct a new world. We are both the influencers and the inspired. We are beings of a cohesive whole."

One day all the amazing heart-centered communities around the globe will ultimately become *one* intentional world community. As visionaries, leaders, and co-creators keep dreaming bigger. Let spirit drive. It's all a domino effect. So keep tilting your heart toward the force of All That Is. May you each find the inspiration and support you need to be dynamic, devoted and imaginative co-creators of new community. You are here to realize that you are the creators of heaven on earth. We at New Village 22 are holding a loving vision of your wondrous participation and success.

In love and radiance,
Melissa, Gabriele, Paula and Barbara

Acknowledgments

All books take a village to create. In this case, this is literally true, as without New Village 22 members there would be no collective manifestation process to report on. I am happily indebted to the love, courage, and support of Gabriele Neumann, Paula Russell, and Barbara Krauss for saying "Yes!" to this remarkable journey and for helping to birth this book. Also, Paula contributed her brilliant editor skills, and Gabriele and Barbara provided their invaluable review and insights throughout.

I am indebted to many loving friends. The consistent intellectual, emotional and spiritual support I receive from them, and my sister Terri Hoopes, make all the difference, all the time. They are the soul-sisters that cheer me along no matter what. I'm so lucky to have connected to them in this lifetime. Also, I include my clients as dear friends. Thank you for making me smarter and wiser, and for helping me to grow. I am honored to have your trust.

My thanks to Suzanna Gratz who provided two great Northern California locations for me to occupy during the initial writing of this book. I so needed to be free of distractions and the January sunshine was an added bonus. Maureen St. Germaine, Wendy Lynne and Margit Crane generously read the first draft of this book and gave me invaluable input that undoubtedly make this a more enjoyable book for you to read. Patricia Duff was also an editing angel who gave the manuscript one last look.

Thank you to all the remarkable people who agreed to be interviewed and who "inhabit" this book as an enriching chorus of community voices. My love to all wise bloggers, authors, channels, teachers, and leaders — the women and men who inspire me, and who continue to do remarkable work in the world to uplift humanity, shift consciousness, and help elevate one another through this remarkable life ride we are on! This includes Julie Umpleby, Sarah Varcas, Lucia Rene, Nora Herold, Wendy Kennedy, Hazel Courteney, Alan Seale, Deepak Chopra, Barbara Marx Hubbard, Tom Kenyon, Marianne Williamson, Marci Shimoff, Anodea Judith, and many more. And, my deep love and appreciation to all our guides unseen, who keep leaving us bread crumbs to follow, and who usher in remarkable wisdom, insight and magic.

All my love and gratitude to my sweet and generous husband, Tracy Sisley. Without his support it simply would not have been possible to focus on this project so completely and to finish it in such a timely manner. His enduring love, good humor, embrace of my various communities, and belief in me just make life more joyous and harmonious. He is my first community always.

Thank you to the wonderful and loving people who helped to crowdfund this project. Your financial and energetic support was paramount to manifesting the book. You are:

Joyce Anderson	Grace O'Malley	Mary Mallon	Anna Shatrova
Paula Russell	Janice Williams	Rosie Dunn	Kristiina Huikka
Zita Gustin	Phoebe Patten	Kris Steinnes	Lily & Lee Lei
Tina Schaaf	Elaine Chan	Gabriele Neumann	Spiros Lappas
Betsy Moore	Sharlyn Hidalgo	Susan Dolan	John Dolan
Joanie Hirshman	Brenda Reynolds	Kim Thoreson	Theresa Day
Tara Gimmer	Mara Davidson	Silvia E. Reed	Maureen St. Germain
Barbara Krauss	Nicole Martin	India Holden	Suzanne Anderson
Margit Crane	Tracy Sisley	Stacy Willoughby	Becky Sisley

Appendix 1: Manifestation Symbols

This is a compilation of the symbols we received in our intuitive processes over a year period that may be helpful to your own understanding of symbols, and what you notice and receive as visual language. In addition, you can use dream symbol books to learn more. I highly recommend Ted Andrew's book *Animal Speak* to learn about animal symbols.

Black and white. Full spectrum frequency (polar frequencies working together like a piano keyboard).

Blue and white (in patterns/fabric, overall coloring). New blueprint.

Blue globe of light. Universal growth potential/seeded wisdom/divine feminine. Has a healing essence.

Breathing under water. Trusting the breath.

Circle portal. Earth passageway for energy.

Clay. Represents the energy of an idea. When we create, ideas are the basic building material.

Convertible. Transition vehicle that moves forward from momentum already established.

Desert. An energetic space between communities. Space for unfolding possibility. "Empty" boundless growth space where all possibility exists.

Diamond. The diamond is the structure representing the new unfolding of our higher potential through the heart mind. Cooperation and feedback are the main principles of the diamond in geomancy.

Diving. Willingness to go deeper into multidimensional experience.

Drop Zone: Place or space to ground energy and to establish alignment with earth.

Eagle. Symbolic for action and focus at work. The eagle is invoked for revitalization, creation and healing purposes.

Earth. Mother of new community. Heart-exchange energy source. Co-creative partner.

Estuary/Ocean. Divine spirit from which all is birthed; it is the womb where we merge with and nourish our higher-self wisdom; a message about creating the right environment here on Earth for "richer, more nutrient-dense" living to take place (fulfillment).

Fairy. Spirit of community potential coming into form.

Fireworks. Expansive energy and energetic downloads from cosmic sources. Indicates breakthrough insights and knowing — neurons firing with new connections of understanding. Indication that Higher Self is awakening personal consciousness.

Flying. Catching air, lift-off. All symbolic of movement, progress of getting off the ground with our project, of our beginnings. Air is also a symbol for mental intelligence and creativity (A reminder perhaps that we are nourished and affected by the elements: fire, water, earth, air).

Four-petal flower. Balance of elements and four directions. It is the unity of the parts that creates the beauty of the whole. Any combination of individual elements/people will create something entirely new with its own essence and momentum.

Girl as feminine divine and **boy** as masculine divine at a "young" stage.

Kite feels much like successfully surfing the waves of emotional energy. May indicate riding thought currents or currents of higher vision. Being the Kite itself may indicate oneness with expanded vision, with a "refreshing" and uplifted perspective, a kind of going with the flow.

Illuminated circle in triangle. Portal of illumination. Access point for community spirit that is surrounded by creative energy. The energy that flows from this circle may be transmitted through one's heart. Members of community foster and protect their own community spirit (don't let outside influences derail their enthusiasm).

Island/oasis of light. Elemental "centers" generating enlightenment energy. Individuals embodying light, and attracting others to them.

Jumping. Making a fearless leap into the unknown with purpose and direction.

Kite. Vehicle for riding thought currents or downloads of higher vision. Being the Kite itself may indicate oneness with expanded vision, with a refreshing and uplifted perspective. Extremely powerful mental flow.

Light dome (white waiting room). A holding space and (intensifier) for gestation/germination of community.

Lineage (lines of people). Represents family and spiritual heritage. Reminder that we come to the world as part of a group and act in this world connected to that group energy. We are never truly alone.

Lotus. Unfolding of our highest powers and potential, how our soul unfolds itself heart, mind, and body. The energies of Earth and Spirit manifesting as One.

Merging waves. Illustrates how energy, color, sound, movement and so forth merge and come together as one. How opposites merge back into one Source. Mimic sound waves.

Moon. Signals indirect or intuitive wisdom one is receiving.

Pastel colors. Signal initial manifesting energy that flows out into the world gracefully, without strain. Pastel colors carry daytime energy, blooming energy.

Puma. Ancient wisdom that supports new knowledge. Represents dawning of new understanding, growth and discovery. Solar animal that enlivens these qualities through daily activity.

River. Life progress (flow). Carrier of life energy, and life itself.

Roller coaster. Signals ability to ride (ride out) emotional waves and intense waves of energy that come to Earth.

Salt water. Nutrient-rich, cleansing and healing environment. A natural component of a buoyant spirit.

Second trimester. Second cycle of community development/collective manifestation.

Sheriff. Protector-translator of new "laws of the land."

Snakes. Symbols for the wisdom of all-knowing Earth. Serpents remind us that we are on a journey to integrate into our consciousness who we truly are. The snakes invites us to create a world where all these energies of nature can live in harmony with each other — by holding space for male/female, darkness/light, science/spirit, silence/sound, art/logic et cetera to co-exist.

Sound. Force of creation that can be used in everyday creativity and spiritual practice. (Also, a body of water where vibrations carry easily.)

Sparkles in water. Sign of presence/atmosphere of expansive energy.

Sun. Father of new community. Energy of feminine divine.

Surfing. Riding waves of energy during various phases of manifestation. Ups and downs, highs and lows are natural. Phases include: pausing on shore to observe a situation before jumping in; doing the initial work of creating momentum by paddling out to the waves; riding the wave of energy and keeping one's balance, and being back on shore joyful and satisfied with the experience.

Triangle. Symbolic of feminine, spirituality, fire, creation. Two triangles indicate integration of masculine and feminine. Triangle can also refer to any threesome: past-present-future, beginning-center-end, mother-father-child, girl-woman-crone, mind-body-spirit.

Underwater treasure. Gems of growth from diving into emotions, into flow of life, and going deeper into spirit. Can choose when to dive for the gems. Launching points for transformation.

Waterfall/river. Fresh energy coming from multiple sources (many rivers/streams feed a waterfall).

White Bubble. Incubator (like a cocoon) that holds essence until person/process takes another form.

Willow tree. According to Sharlyn Hidalgo, author of *The Healing Power of Trees: Spiritual Journey's Through the Celtic Tree Calendar*, willows are found near water and relate to feminine power, cooperation, fertility, creativity, the moon, community interest, shared power, the reflected light of the sun, reception, and peace and harmony of the collective. During the meditation the wood oval was an inner passageway too, thus suggesting the many layers of inner being-ness that exist like the many rings you find in a tree trunk (its core).

Womb. Space being held for community development. Safe environment where new community can emerge.

Woodland clearing (glade). Sacred space, an empty entry/reception point.

Appendix 2: New Village 22 Meditation Summaries

Meditation #1: (see chapter 14)

Meditation #2 setup:

Intention to know about "opening portals" and how our process is connected to this. As Gabriele said, "We are three women, each of us holding a specific energy. It would be helpful to know how to anchor what flows through us." The fact that there are three of us reminds Gabriele of the three women who took part in her Create-Compassion Meditations (a series of remote and synchronous meditations to raise consciousness and compassion on Earth conducted from December 2010 to October 2013), and of the three women in Lucia Rene's fascinating book, *Unplugging the Patriarchy*. This synchronicity alerted us to paying attention to the significance three people holding space for manifestation.

Melissa:

The three of us run through the sand dunes joyfully. We sense that we are grounding new energy. A giant keyhole appears illuminated with light. I sense the words: "Going Home...all beings prepare the path. Be one self; be one love system. Earth rejoices. I intuit that Gabriele represents home, hearth and love. Paula represents ancient wisdom and supports with knowledge. I lead this process.

Gabriele:

Sees us sitting far above Earth in lotus position and forming a triangle in which we each sit on a column of light that comes up out of the earth. We are laughing and enjoying the process. A holographic diamond/rhombus is created, and is mirrored until it spreads out over the universe as a 3D body. Our triangle is likewise mirrored until there is the sense that "substance" has been created. A ritual hand movement is enacted that conveys that from heart to heart love energy spreads outward. This is the portal of the heart.

Gabriele asks about the energies we contribute to or represent in this system. She gets the visuals of: flying eagle for Melissa (felt the qualities of focus, big view, sharp eye, effortlessness and spheres); observing puma for Paula (felt the energy of cleverness, really fast but still with lightness, focus for detail), two coiled up snakes for herself. Senses energy spiraling upwards and feels forward propelling energy.

From meditation #2 we learned that:

* We can align with animal symbols.

* Permission dance of first meditation was followed by Gabriele's ritual for heart expansion in this meditation. This willingness to engage ritual as part of the transformation process feels important.

* Being one love system is essential.

* Keyhole appears as a symbol for a significant portal opening/opportunity.

* The concept of Earth and intentional community intertwined as a manifestation of love.

Meditation #3 setup: *"Go swimming in the river. Fly in the falls. Wash free from all obstacles and hindrances. Sing like sirens and play. You will meet your helpers in this glade."*

Melissa's meditation report:

We are playing in a glade around a waterfall pool. As we swim, laugh, float, ride the waterfall, I set the intention to release all that's not needed. We are only immersed in the pool a short while before we get out, giving thanks to the Earth.

Then we are running like children holding hands as we circle around one side of the pool. Suddenly, we lift off like Peter Pan, flying above grey clouds and a red and gold sunset. In my mind, I want us to land, but there is no sense that we are going to. The thought pops into my head: "You are ahead of schedule, plenty of time to land this plane (plan?)." I'm peaceful even as I recognize that I'm in a "holding" pattern. I intuitively ask what we need to do to further the foundation of the village. I receive: "Build the heart bridges." So I focus on being in my heart and building joyful love energy. I send love and light to my companions.

Gabriele's meditation report:

We sit in a wooden boat on a very "juicy" little river in a green and lush landscape. Paddling along, we pass a beautiful glade with woods behind it. I see how the sunlight is reflected from the water and how it breaks into thousands of little sparkles. The river pours into a natural pool, and a waterfall is also filling the pool with fresh water. The three of us swim and laugh. We dive and it's like living underwater, where oxygen is no problem. We climb out of the pool, and I receive the words, "Follow the waterfall." We walk through the waterfall and find a little stream running down the other side of the pool, guiding us to a wooden form.

I sense the wooden form is from a willow tree. It is oval shaped and lying lengthwise. The three of us sit in this wooden vehicle in lotus position, one behind the other. I see spiraling energy in the woods around us, and suddenly the wooden oval is upright. The spirals look like two strands of rainbow colored DNA. We stay like this until the process feels complete.

We get out of the wooden oval near a little stream flowing down the mountains in front of us. It is impossible for us to follow this stream because of the great mountains — but somehow it does not matter. Through a mountain pass I see an empty space where the mountains end and a desert begins.

I ask my spirit guides to be taken to a timeline where a physical form of our community already exists (has been manifested). I see years counting down, it jumps, from 2069 down to 2022, where it stops. Pythagoras comes to mind reminding me that a city ideally has all three main shapes, round, triangle and quadrant, to keep balance and harmony. I get visuals of very happy moments of my life spent in this great community with friends and family.

Feedback from Paula:

Although I wasn't able to join in this meditation, here are a few thoughts after reading both of your notes.

First, I'm happy that both of your visions included me. There's lot of information (and beauty) to digest here, and naturally, I found my position in each quite interesting. I am accustomed to leading and being in charge, whether I want to or not, and generally forging ahead, turning ideas into reality. This has always required a strong focus on the practical while holding the vision. This project feels quite different to me. It's more of a blending of gifts, skills, talents, and desires and an unfolding rather than a forging. It is much softer and gentler without simply disintegrating into vapor with no practical result. I feel no need to focus on the concrete at the moment or to try too hard to make something happen.

Occupying the middle feels like the stabilizing position, and perhaps the force that silently says, "Keep flying, no rush to land." In Gabriele's meditation, I am the one without a paddle, exerting no force. We pass a glade, which is the word I use for my inner meditation place of beauty. We can breathe with ease underwater, which seems to me to mean that we have the necessary inner/outer resources to flow and proceed smoothly — as long as we just breathe where we are. Pythagoras created a community and sacred geometry is one of my deepest interests. Finally, as I write now, I keep hearing the repeated Italian word *"piano, piano"* which means softly, slowly, gently, no rush.

Meditation #4 setup:

We begin by skydiving into the New Village 22 "drop zone" — the energetic location where our community mission will be grounded and anchored.

Melissa's meditation report:

I did this meditation twice. In the first meditation, the three of us jump from the plane. No fear at all. We are playful and holding hands; we are at ease as we descend and fly through the ether. We pull our rip cords and float to earth. We land easily, like superheroes, in the form a triangle. We give thanks for dropping into our zone. I want to go off and explore, but I realize we are meant to stay to acclimatize ourselves to the vibration of this land, so that we will recognize it later. We lie on our backs, heads together and waves of vibration wash over us. We thank this place for its mission of receiving and grounding our physical community into reality. We turn over to so that this earth can receive our heart resonance. It feels as though this will ease the way to establishing relationship with the physical location.

In the second meditation we jump from the plane joyfully, playfully, doing air rolls and whatever strikes our fancy on the way down. No need for parachutes this time. We just land easily and gracefully. I sense "red ground." I see myself walking the parameter of our place, like pacing off land or surveying the property. As I'm doing this I sense two triangles, point-to-point, in the middle of the landscape. (Later, Paula tells me that walking off the parameter is the way the Romans used to measure city boundaries.)

Paula's meditation report:

Jumping from the plane we are laughing and holding hands. This is gleeful and easy. We slow as we get closer to the ground, floating down to earth like Mary Poppins. I see rolling hills, no trees. We gather up the parachutes. We are looking around and I am pointing things out.

Gabriele's meditation report:

I sense us at the plateau in the lush mountain landscape of our last meditation. It's night, and we perform a happy "circle dance" ritual. I sense a fourth person, but the person is not clear. The dance feels like a dance women performed in the moonlight to increase fertility in ancient times. The scene changes and we are back in space above the Earth, forming a triangle. We laugh, have fun, and we pray together. After finishing the ritual and our prayer we are back on the mountain plateau and three air jets appear. It's an adventure! We are turning somersaults and we jump on flying ladders that the jets have prepared for us to come on board — very much James Bond style. The jets race off to the desert space we saw from the mountain plateau. We jump off the jets here. Jumping is not an issue as we just jump and somehow arrive back on Earth. A blinding light awaits us. Out of this light a group of cosmonauts or astronauts come walking towards us in slow motion. They are wearing full space suits and helmets in white. I receive the words: *"The technology is invented right now."* This reminds me of the inner technologies/heart technologies/5D technology we have been hearing about from channel Wendy Kennedy about how to work with the new energy coming in. Old energy technologies not working anymore — we invent our own technology right here, right now! The technology for what? I can't answer this question.

Meditation #5 setup: We will go to the area where we parachuted last meditation. We'll be planting sacred intention seeds for the fruition of our community. Intentions include:

* *I allow open space in my heart/energy field for fresh visions to seed themselves.*

* *I plant seeds for global plenty.*

* *I intend for wholeness and unity to pollinate among all players who join in this endeavor.*

* *I intend that a strong and lasting energy foundation be established for the easy unfolding of our community.*

We acknowledge that we are not alone in this seed planting — that there are unseen partners now joining us. These seeds help to focus our growth and manifestation, as well as affirm humanity's growth and manifestation around the world.

Melissa's meditation report:
I began the meditation as a quick review of where we are — like a movie being fast forwarded. I sense the ground rushing up to meet me. I'm rolling around on the ground to receive and exchange energy signals with the land very playfully.

I connect my heart with Gabriele and Paula. I have a white linen bag full of seeds. I open it first for Gabriele. I expect that she is going to take lots of seeds, but she takes just a bare handful saying that her energy-work magic will make these seeds go far. Paula takes two handfuls saying that she will "hold" these in reserve for future plantings. I think that I'm going to plant slowly with focus on each seed, but suddenly I become a human "seed" sprinkler — spinning and sending the seeds flying out of the bag. This is quite joyous and fun. I think about my intentions as this is happening.

Then the three of us join hands in a line walking forward across the seeded land radiating high energy. The scenery rushes by us, much as it feels when riding in a convertible car. Then we are holding hands and running into the ocean...then climbing a rocky mountain...then bounding up into the trees. Finally I stand on a pile of seeds invoking the prayer, "By sunlight and moonlight these seeds will be nourished and bloom as one seed: the village whole. Amen."

Gabriele's meditation report:
First I see a lot of bubbles flying around in space, like the blue and magenta faces Melissa intuitively painted after the last meditation. I recognize them as my cosmonauts and the second I realize this, the bubbles change shape and become the cosmonauts again. This time, there are many of them, like an army of cosmonauts, all dressed in those typical white spacesuits, holding a helmet under one arm. I receive the words *"walking the ground."* (Melissa was walking the parameter in an earlier meditation and walking the field with us in this one.)

I ask in what ways I can use my frequency for the good of the New Village 22 project. I am told to hold New Village 22 frequency in my right hand and to hold my frequency (standing for love, beauty & compassion) in my left hand, which I do. Through my heart, I am the connector of these two energies; there is nothing to do, just to be. As I feel these energies in my hands, I slowly sense them as eternal energy pillars. Now the energy is flowing from left to right through my heart effortlessly. Then I am told to form a triangle by making prayer position in front of my heart chakra, and then to form a ball with the energy. So I open my hands to feel the energy between my palms. Slowly I feel it getting stronger until thee energy ball is about 20 centimeters in diameter. This energy glows a beautiful blue light. I feel a strong, but gentle energy and glowing coming from this energy ball. After the ball has summoned enough energy that it feels complete, I am told to plant this ball in Holy Earth. I see dark, fertile soil. It is night and the full moon is glowing. I dig a deep hole, put the energy ball inside, and cover it.

Now I sense Melissa and Paula near me. We perform a dancing ritual while holding hands. In the glowing moonlight there are fairies flying about, celebrating with us. The more we dance the more it feels like flying until we are flying through the glowing moonlight and blue light. We land safe and sound inside the wooden oval shape (of the last meditation), which is again standing vertical and reminds me of a birth channel made out of wood. We land, feeling like we did a good job!

—∞∞—

Meditation #6 setup:

The intention is to begin with a baptism/purification of the village. This includes washing with water and nourishing the seeded environment with a flow of our respective high energies.

Melissa's meditation report:

First, I saw us on the land where we left off sprinkling seeds. We sat positioned as we were in the corners of a triangle — facing each other and sending each other our respective "land" frequency energy. Then we sat back-to-back sending out nourishing energy to all corners of the seeded land (a kind of sending energy inward and outward). From wooden bowls we ladle water onto the earth like a baptism and watering intention at the same time. I am inspired to silently chant the Kadosh, Kadosh, Kadosh, Adonai Tsebayoth refrain (roughly translated as: Holy, Holy, Holy is the Lord God, the whole Earth is full of his glory). According to the teachings of Maureen St. Germain, this chant creates a clearing and a space so holy that we can feel the presence of Divine. Then I close the ceremony by giving thanks to All That Is.

Gabriele's meditation report:

I see us sitting around a campfire on the mountain plateau, but only for short while. Immediately the scene changes and I see my Higher Self in a bubble of white light gliding through space/time. I sense that I am floating towards my "dream home." Suddenly Terra X — Estrine (a star system I am encouraged to communicate with, originating from my last personal meditation) comes to my mind, and I feel a "click." Estrine or estuaries seems to point to a connection with water, or a connection with the magical beings of the water. I am in my dream home with my Higher Self. Here everything just feels right; all makes sense.

I ask, "What is the next best step for the village project?" Answer: "There is no next step; there is only facilitating, allowing in, and aligning with the unfolding process." So I ask, "What am I allowed to facilitate today?" Since Friday I've had a painful muscle cramp in my left shoulder that is calling for attention. I am asked to breathe into the pain in my shoulder. While breathing, a blue energy ball in my shoulder starts to grow bigger, encompassing the painful area. I sense that I am to open up to all the wisdom and knowledge that wants to flow through me. Then I am asked to open my hand to let in the magical blue light. It feels as I if am receiving my frequency colors. I sense how the blue light moves up through my arm to the place with the pain in my left shoulder. Also, I am asked to open my other hand to allow the blue light to circulate. Then I sense an energy ball in front of my heart chakra. It feels much like the energy ball/energy seed I put into the earth during our intention seeding. I am asked to direct the blue energies to this energy seed. I sense that somehow the blue energy is connected to water energy, as I sense the words "a treasure can be retrieved from water." I receive the idea to bless the energy ball in front of me with the words, "I bless you with the 'I AM.'" I say this three to four times. This feels much like giving the baby a name during a baptism ceremony. The second this ceremony feels complete, the energy ball changes and an angel appears. The angel has white/golden colors and has a large presence.

I ask, "Who are you?"
The angel says, "I am the Village Angel."
"Are you the Spirit of the Village place?"
"No! "
"Are you the Spirit of the Village project?"
"No, not yet. I am here to be modified; I am like the clay out of which you make a beautiful statue or vase or plate. I am summoned energy of an idea."

Then I see our six frequency colors as light columns that create a hexagon. This shape is the opened meditation "room" in which we create our community. I sense the information, "The room is open, you open and close with intention."

Paula meditation report:
I live on a plateau, and in thinking about the phrase "pagan places of peace," that Melissa got in her Akashic Records reading, I kept seeing a woodland clearing, very beautiful, like an outdoor "cathedral" or magic fairy spot. I feel very connected to you both and our community project, and have a sense of being kind of a counter-balance to you. Not so much like a practical force in opposition to the metaphysical, but as an adjunct and kind of actual space holder. Maybe like the person who holds the kite and delights in its flight.

This morning in meditation I kept feeling an overwhelming sense of well-being and non-urgency — as if all is well and unfolding as it should. At times I was swimming in lovely deep warm water with my eyes open, breathing easily, and lots of sparkling twinkling lights (treasures?) below. I felt no need to investigate them at that moment, but was happy to know they are there.

⸙

Meditation #7 setup:

Enter our meditation room with the intention to ask or experience what we can know about sounding.

Gabriele meditation report:

As I connect with the theme of sound and today's full moon, a scene from the fourth Harry Potter movie, *Harry Potter and the Goblet of Fire*, circulates through my mind. Specifically the scene in which Harry takes a golden egg with him into a bath to find out what the "noise" is about when he opens the golden egg. Above water when opening the egg there is only a terrible screeching. Yet, underwater he hears a wonderful voice singing. This reminds me of the voice of a mermaid. I stay "in tune" and receive the information that underwater cosmic tunes are better understood. Also, a baby is in fluid for nine months receiving "worldly and cosmic tunes" during the gestation period. I receive, "Invite beneficial tunes/cosmic sounds into the village baby belly." I sense a connection to the estuary theme that came up in the last meditation. Our first meditation started on a river (an analogy for conception?) and we have reached the estuary (gestation time). The waters in an estuary create a fertile mixture (sweet water/salt water might be an analogy for Earthly tunes/cosmic tunes or energies). Perhaps estuary is a symbol for mixing within the life-giving ocean of All That Is. I sense: "Listen to the cosmic tunes under water; here they are much better translated than above water." At this point this information feels complete.

Next I ask, "What is our process for this full moon? Where are we in our process?" Suddenly I see Melissa carrying heavy stones. She has built a round form/device out of these stones with about a 1.5 meter diameter (stone on stone, all stones are round). She has built them up to the height of her hips. I join her and want to understand what she is doing, but suddenly the whole form/device starts to build itself and grows into the sky. It is night, and there is a portal made out of moonlight. It feels like a cosmic portal, some lightning also visible. The two of us are still standing on the ground. I ask, "What is my part here?" I sense that my part is to tune the device, and that I need to touch it with my hands. So I put my hands around it, allowing the energy from my hands to flow into the stone formation. The energy starts to swirl and spiral upwards, and the formation starts to look like a thread of DNA. I sense Paula inside the device and get the information that Paula is the one holding the energy from the inside. I receive the idea that Melissa changes/transforms the "building material" of the device as necessary. Finally, the idea that New Village 22 points to the 22nd century drops into my awareness, and that this is the creation of a new blueprint, a city of light.

Melissa's meditation reports:

I was inspired to begin the meditation yesterday (a day ahead of the full moon). Again, I had the awareness we don't have to exactly coordinate in time/space, rather we coordinate our connection through intention. For this meditation focused on sound, I decide to chant "Love Om" (a theme that appeared on a dream board). I started by generating energy/frequency in the palms of my hands. I chant OM from softly to loudly, feeling the tones in different chakras. This felt very primal. I didn't try to direct anything I just opened my mouth and let sound come out, whatever tone wanted to be created. Felt like an ancient wise woman both calling in the sacred and answering a sacred call (the in and out flow again). This primal call was a receiving and sending out of energy. I sent out this sacred sound energy in all directions. It was like those movie special effects in which you can see the waves of energy moving outward (like from an explosion, only very gently in this case). It felt natural seeing what we don't usually perceive. As I write this I sense that indeed it will become more natural to see energy in addition to feeling it. I was both in the sound and creating a sound field. I was establishing the ground for a "force field" from which structures can arise. I see the three of us sitting cross-legged facing each other. We are chanting OM and we bow in at the waist and then lean backward. As I see this in my mind I bend forward at my waist in my chair and keep chanting. This feels sacred, like an ancient persona I am remembering to call in the forces of nature and the divine.

Melissa's second meditation report:

I'm back at the landing site where I "walked off" the property and we planted the seeds of intention. Knowing that I did initial "sound" work yesterday, I look at the field, at what is germinating. Suddenly I am in the field raising a structure (like metal work in the early stages of a building) with a loud OM that is more like the sound that Don Knotts made in the movie, *The Incredible Mr. Limpet*. The metal struts don't come straight out of the ground to form a square; the shape is more like an inverted trapezoid (a structure to be filled up, perhaps, or to hold collected energy). In our field it's a structure that is germinating. This structure that we are raising is like a "ghost" structure. It is energetically present, although not firmly actualized as of yet, but this is a necessary step. I send out a powerful sound.

Then I am down by the ocean watching dolphins and a whale jumping. There are tall trees near the beach. I "sound out" the faeries, elves and other glade spirits with an, "Olly, Olly oxen free, free, free" like I called as a kid playing hide and seek. This is meant to let these "supporting" spirits know that it's safe to come out and show themselves. I remember that we are a permission-based village, so I ask the trees for permission to erect structures in their branches and they bend in approval. I ask the mountains if we may erect structures within their majesty and I see them smile. I do the same for the fields. I experience this as a joyous process of bringing *all* energies into "the fold" of the village project.

Meditation #8 setup: Intention is to know about how to use creativity to access deeper meaning and information about creating community. This intention is based on information that I receive from an Akashic Record reading that transmitted the following:

One-World One-Reality is in the works. Collective consciousness is in creative array and in peace. Abstract aspects are no longer emotionally dominant. Drama is no longer the differentiator. Creative purpose is the differentiator, the drive. It's not how dramatic life is, it's how creatively inspired and transpired. The play is The Sun and The Moon, and all The Stars in formation. The Yin and The Yang aligned into powerful force. Black and White vibrating as all colors of the rainbow at once. Vibration is the playing field — the frequency field of play. Practice and proceed, no wrong way to start. Choose destination and play with the joy of your frequency. Bring that to bear and all is well. Worry not the details until they appear.

Melissa's meditation report:

We are sitting crossed legged in our field, facing each other. We greet one another lovingly. Our palms are on the ground. Suddenly we are levitating a few feet up, from the energy of our palms being directed into the earth. Then, I'm not conscious of you two. I'm facing the "ghost" structure that I raised in my last meditation. I transform the ghost structure's metal beams into a rounded "wave" building. I start speaking my wishes into the walls of this building from the inside (and simultaneously into all walls/structures of the village that will exist). I project joy, love and excitement energy into the walls and structures. I'm then aware that a Dome of Light is over the entire village. This Dome of Light incubates and creates connection to the heavens — to the cosmos. I see only the glowing top of the Dome. Above me a night sky full of stars is slowly spinning. It's beautiful and serene.

Gabriele's meditation report:

I see the picture of a pregnant woman in three gestation periods — the trimesters. I perceive that the first trimester has come to a close. Now we are transcending into the second phase. This reminds me how a baby develops in amniotic fluid during these periods. In the beginning "fish like" (like a heart with eyes), which then reminds me of the water pictures and the estuary scenes which popped up during my last meditations (when I was told about sounds under water). In the second period of a pregnancy the baby starts more and more to shape into what it is about to become, limbs, gender, and so on become more developed.

Then suddenly the scene changes and I see the three of us in a dark golden convertible car. The roof is open as we drive along a very long and straight road (reminds me of transition) towards rocky mountains (reminds me of form and shape) through an empty, desert-like landscape. None of us is driving as the car is driven by an invisible force. We laugh and really have fun during this drive.

Again the scene changes and now we are in a white waiting room. There are lots of empty chairs along the walls. In the middle of the room there is a table with a white architectural model of a city on it. We walk around this table in a kind of ritualistic way, and while we watch the model it changes shape from rectangular to round. So interesting that this happens while we watch (like quantum physics concept that observation influences the outcome).

⸻

Meditation # 9 setup:

We set a simple intention to know what is next for New Village 22.

Melissa's meditation report:

I did an Akashic Records reading rather than a meditation. (see chapter 15)

Gabriele meditation report:

I'm inspired to light a candle for this meditation and find a purple water candle in a little magenta bowl with a golden heart at its bottom. I recall that we are in the time of Easter/East, which in geomancy is represented by water and the archetypical sign "ᴗ" (like a bowl). My bowl filled with water felt a little like an offering to the "forces of the East" (symbolizing the egg, spring, birth, life forces coming back) to come and join me in this meditation. As I lit the candle I thought: "The candle represents fire & West. In geomancy fire connotes action, and power. So I also felt like inviting the forces of the West and of fire to show us the way into the next step (action). East and West form a horizontal line, which signals getting broader and wider (versus higher/deeper). All of this I realized a few moments before I started meditating.

Meditation:

This time, I intentionally invited in the Spirit of the Village. I ask the Spirit: "How are you?"

Answer: "A bit formless yet." I sense no form or shape yet, but an essence. I get the impulse to put the Spirit of the Village in front of my inner vision and ask for its name. I sense an "A." Then I ask the Spirit of the Village: "What can I do for you today? What do you request?" Answer:

257

"Send me your light, your energy each day for 45 days to nurture and to give me form!" I ask how much time we should spend sending our light-energy frequency. Felt like a short intentional setting of about two minutes. I invite all spirit guides of the village to assist us in this. I send my energy through my hands to the village. The energy goes in vertical and horizontal circles around the cloud-like village formation. Then within the cloud I suddenly see a boy on the left and a girl on the right around age six in black and white (frequency symbol). They are standing back-to-back in a white bubble (protected essence without form) looking at me. I am still sending them energy. I get the sense that they are twins and they represent divine masculine and divine feminine.

Then I ask the Spirit of the Village if there is a wish for energy clearing? Answer: "Yes." So I call upon Archangel Michael and Raphael. I don't really see a lot, but sense some shifts. I get the impulse to ask both of you if you want some clearing, and both of you agree. I sense some beings around you performing the clearing. I see that you, Melissa, look like a vase in which the water level goes lower and lower, leaving the vase shining and sparkling. Paula, you were helping to clear your own energy system. You were using your arms and hands to push energy down, away and out of your system. After this treatment all my inner visuals were much clearer and brighter. There was a very beautiful moment when I suddenly sensed very clearly you, Paula, next to me, smiling, laughing, and shiny. Together we made the celebratory gesture of "Give me five!" At this moment I had the feeling and thought: "This is how it's going to be when we meet for the first time in real life." Some tears and warm sensations in my body came up. (Our group gathers remotely, and the four of us have not yet met in physical reality since Gabriele lives in London.) I asked why this clearing was necessary, and got the answer that it is normal and a good idea to clear from time to time as all absorbs lower energies, fear and doubt.

Meditation #10 setup:

The intention is to meet in the village energy field to enlarge vision and to expand the inner self and outer space for playing with new possibilities.

Melissa's meditation report:

The first nine meditations established the energetic ground for community. I decide to intuitively ask questions.

Q: "What are the next 10 steps of cycle two?"
A: 1.   Refresh perspective
   2.   Hold space for more possibility
   3.   Shake off setbacks
   4.   Believe in peace
   5.   Create a true model form
   6.   Write it to the world
   7.   Begin construction in mind
   8.   Begin creative design in play
   9.   Invite new members
   10.   Begin anew cycle three

Q: Is the New Village 22 missing any critical components at this time/cycle of development?

A: Yes, peace of mind. It helps to focus on that. Let it wash through all phases, wash through, wash through. Then the building energy will hold. There are enough points on the grid to ensure eventual manifestation. More ideas are needed to be fleshed out to bring new light into project. Travel will help this.

As part of the intent to "refresh" our perspective, Paula and I go to visit the Snoqualmie Falls (270-foot waterfall located outside of Seattle, Washington) running at their full majestic power at this time. We take a few minutes to sit and "receive" while waves of misty breezes from these thunderous falls washes over us.

Paula's meditative impressions at the falls:

I received impressions of polar opposites existing in harmony and providing healing energy. Felt I was plugging in and recharging to:

* Warmth and sun along with cool clouds and mist (revitalizing synergy).

* Loud and soft.

* Huge power flow and stillness.

* Trees rooted and ease of water flowing down.

* Powerful and gentle.

* Energizing and relaxing.

Melissa's meditative impressions at falls:

Earth is moving, flowing like molten lava down a hillside. Every grain is in action, in movement. There is expansion and recharging.

Based on my (nighttime) dreams about old interior walls being removed, I set the intention to push out the new energetic walls of the village as far as they want to go...going beyond...beyond. I asked for ideas of form to flow to me, and see the earthen flow going through me.

Second meditation:

Again have the impression of expansion of territories. I'm flying over the New Village 22 at a fast clip — like a giant kite fluttering in the wind. Fluttering wings of material are blowing in the breeze. I bring my heart into alignment with the heart of the village. I set the intention again for the New Village 22 to be a place of joy, excitement, peace and cooperation. (With all the drama of my brother's life this past week, I felt I wanted to reinforce these qualities.)

Gabriele's meditation report:
Only saw a huge heart made out of fireworks.

—∞∞∞—

Meditation #11 setup:
Intention is to put something concrete on the energetic grid. This could be an invention of some kind; it could be a structure that you would like to see in the village; it could be something that reflects our core values like environmental responsibility. I sense that somehow living what we want, right now, grounds our "elevated" vision/idea/ invention into the energetics of the village foundation. Living it now helps to bring the spirit mind down to earth. We can authentically communicate with others about this centered community vision, as we continue to ground various possibilities.

Melissa's meditation report:
I invoke the village grid and visualize adding a layout of round houses. I invite in our village pillars of creativity, learning and energy. I ring my meditation bell three times. I invite in the energy of ideal transportation for the village. Then I get the idea to accept the blueprints for New Village 22 from the Master Architect (All That Is). I ring the bell once. I see myself being very excited to view the blueprints for the village. Also, keep thinking back to Disneyland and the rides because of the emotional roller coaster that I have been on with my brother. Life always presents new opportunities for me to hold my center.

Gabriele's meditation report:

I call in the Spirit of New Village 22. A picture of a beautiful young woman appears in my inner vision wearing a long white "airy fairy" dress (like the woman on Melissa's lunar eclipse dream board). I ask, "How can I be of service today?" I receive the words, *"Everybody who helps in birthing the village gives birth to himself; everybody who helps bringing the potential to earth is the potential himself. Be well grounded."* Then the beautiful woman says, *"I am still so young, but not that formless, not done birthing yet."* Feels like we're in a phase of creation, and there will be additional stages.

Meditation #12 setup: Akashic Records reading

Sound elements have come to the forefront recently. Last week I was down at Discovery Park on the Puget Sound. I was listening to the sound of the lapping water when I had the thought, "I'm in the middle of Surround Sound!" This made me wonder if all the "sound" clues we have been getting are actually clues having to do with sound relating to water. I was also watching the little waves coming in. One big wave would break into two waves and they would roll in towards one another and merge in a criss-cross pattern and get absorbed into oneness. Since I have this pattern showing up on dream boards I wondered about noticing it here. I felt like an observer centered in a sound-scape. These thoughts inspired me to do an Askashic Records reading for New Village 22. Below are my notes:

Q: How do I use sound waves in the creation of New Village 22?

A: You are One with Sound. Sound vibrates, disturbs, distributes energy waves — directs waves of energy. You bring to yourself and others through sound.

Q: What is the best sound for me to use?

A: It is the tune of your heart playing at all times — turned on and up into the atmosphere.

Gabriele comment: Reminds me of "Schumann Resonance" (human brain alpha waves resonate at 7.83 Hz/same as Schumann Frequency of 7.83 Hz, emitted from planet Earth, discovered by Professor W.O. Schumann — especially in relation to heart/mind coherence).

Q: What "sound" instruments assist me in tuning my heart, in bringing heart to its fullest?

A: Be a sound wave. Know that though you look solid, you are a heart sound wave. Breathe that. Be that. You decide the tune. Set your song of the day (Makes me want to pay attention to what "sound tracks" play in my head. On Friday it was "At the Ballet" from A Chorus Line. Yesterday as I was gardening, it was "My Funny Valentine.")

Q: What is Surround Sound?

A: Surround sound is the power to vibrate with all things, all creations, at once. Tune yourself to the vibrations of all living creatures. As you experience your Oneness, your Surround Sound amplifies out into the Universe so that it can be used for the good of the Cosmos.

Q: How do sound waves help me to bring New Village 22 to shore, to ground it in reality?

A: Know your timing is perfect at all times. No way to linger too long or run too fast. Yes, the middle way is perfect. Proceed at will and all goes according to plan. Peace.

Gabriele comment: That is what I thought, that the waves come to shore anyway. The village project will come ashore one day — like a mother who has to wait until the due date to hold her newborn baby. Nature normally takes over and prepares the way. If mother and child are healthy, gravity will do its job to bring the baby into the light.

Q: How do sound waves keep me centered?

A: They resonate and then flow through you. Their own center "pull" keeps you centered. They create that invisible thread that aligns down through the chakras (suddenly song "World on a String" pops into my head...related to string theory?). By feeling into your center you align with world energy "string" — that which wraps around the planet in peace and prosperity.

Q: What may I know about my Higher Self coming in waves?

A: Now you see it...Now you don't. Everything in God's Grace comes in waves...not static...never attempt to *hold* onto energy flow. Rather be One with the flow of energy to allow Higher Self to show up more tangibly.

Gabriele comment: Reminds me that often we think that things are linear, but in truth all comes in circles/cycles and it seems accurate that processes and energy spirals up instead of developing on a line.

Q: What can I understand about energy rising and energy falling?

A: Name not the direction. Feel it — what comes and what goes, passing in both directions. Waves that expand evermore even as they ground back into All That Is.

Q: What is the ground of my being?

A: Light.

Q: What is the best focus or starting point for the next New Village 22 New Moon Meditation?

A: In all things be as One. See the waves of sound running through the village. Center in these sound waves. See what rises to the sound of your heart.

Melissa's meditation report:

I open my meditation and chant. I envision the three of us side by side in the village field. We hold up our hands with palms facing outward — like we are going to give a benediction/blessing. This enables us to send our respective energies outward. Then we are singing "Alleluia." Then singing like birds. I think of robins. A flock of birds circle around the field in a "swoosh" of perfectly orchestrated flow. Now singing like Orca whales that are jumping through the field. We see the waves of sound energy flowing towards us like my description of how the waves came toward me at the Puget Sound: a single wave breaking into two waves and then merging. I invoke financing/a shared economy for the village. I ask that all people receive exactly what they need in perfect timing. To close, I ring the meditation bell for a prolonged interval of about 15 seconds.

Gabriele's meditation report:

The tone of what I experienced in meditation was very smooth, very tranquil, flowing, loving, happy and relaxed, even settled. Had a lovely start as I saw us sitting on the beautiful mountain plateau (may be a home base for me in regards to the village meditations). In the moonlight we sat in lotus position around an equal sided triangle. With hands in prayer position, we were saying invocations or prayers. It did not feel as if we just had come together for this sitting. It felt as if I came along to observe something that was already going on, and that would continue to go on once I left. The amazing thing was that behind each of us I saw lots of "beings" standing in line, our support teams — our lineages! It felt much like all knowledge intuitively flowed through this line into our hands and hearts, into our "aware" knowingness.

Then we sit around something looking like a circular opening in the earth within the triangle. This triangle is full of etheric white glowing light, which comes out of the opening a bit like fog. Rising toward the sky the fog forms a thread looking a bit like DNA, holding this thread is a beautiful young girl who comes up out of the glowing light looking angelic. She is wearing a crown of flowers and is dressed in white (a reference to the white architectural model of the last meditation?). I believe that this might be the Spirit of the Village.

Then for a few moments its feels like dreaming in two dimensions — or getting access to a parallel universe. I am holding/getting the visual of us under the moonlight around the triangle, but at the same time I see this most beautiful child in a kind of garden paradise, playing, laughing, and being so happy. There are no other beings visible, but I don't think that this child feels alone, as there are many companions somehow. I hold these two visuals until only the visual with us around the triangle remains (with the girl still holding onto the thread).

I sense the lineage being very close during these moments, I watch as a magical theatre of alternating moonlight and sunlight dances across the sky. I receive the words: "*With every (energetic) block you move out of your system we (the lineage) move closer and you become more and more aware of our connection. This is your connection with your true lineage, which in fact had never gone. It was only that you were not aware of it, like the connection was distorted. The more you do your personal work the more you free the way for this baby to come through.*"

I ask if there is anything we need to put into motion, but only get the feeling that all is well for now. I get the sense that once things need to be "thought," "done" or "said" that these things will present themselves to us. The order of the day is to do our personal work honestly — processing fears, energetic blocks, anything holding us back. We are to stay focused on whatever we do and pursue with an authentic mind and heart.

Meditation #13 setup:

Intention is to align as one force of potential for community formation. I do an Akashic Record reading to check in with my guides.

Q: What may I know about the realization of New Village 22?

A: Not looking for sameness; diversity is king.

Q: In the next 3 months is there a particular focus that will help bring New Village 22 into form?

A: Imagination:

What can be...

What is beyond belief...

What stays in your minds...

What leaps in the heart...

What plays with right possibilities...

What is just round the corner...

What is just behind the veil of reality that you can glimpse...

Shop possibilities as if it there were an unlimited supply of goods!

Q: Anything else that I, Paula or Gabriele should know about our roles in the village?

A: Be One Heart. Right now running separate tracks of concern. Very Earthly behavior and yet you all can take one step beyond such woes of mind. Ready yourselves for stepping beyond normal — stay not in the realm of past earth. Step up into ascended being. It will take dedication and commitment, discipline of the highest order. Be of joy beyond all else!

Gabriele meditation report:

I call in the Spirit of the Village, all kind-hearted benevolent beings who are with us and I call in our Highest Selves. Again the three of us are on the mountain plateau around the triangle of light in prayer. The difference this time is that we are all pregnant (about five months).

Again, I see the light pillar looking like a thread of rainbow colored DNA spiraling downwards in the center of the triangle and receive the words, "Germinating the world." Colorful fuzz-like pieces come off the spiral and fly out into the dark night. While this happens I see transparent walls growing (made of transparent building blocks) along the sides of the triangle. It begins to look like a transparent pyramid, with the light DNA pillar still spiraling counter-clockwise in the middle. The moment all three walls are complete and meet at the top of the pyramid, I receive the words, "This is the moment the diamond opens." Now I see a diamond on top of the pyramid. I ask what the diamond represents and receive, "The diamond carries the essence, the light of the new world." With these words I also receive the visual of a circle slowing filling up with light.

Final Meditations for Reception Phase:

I am sharing here two meditations that work together and to convey important points about creating form that is in harmony with Earth. The addition of a fourth member positively enlivens the group dynamic as community thrives on new members bringing their brilliance to the game.

New Village 22 Meditation #14: New Moon

Gabriele's meditation report:

From our plateau, I receive that the light opening "allows deep connection with earth." Stars are shining in a clear sky as we greet each other with smiles and invite in all our spirit guides. I see many beings coming towards us, surrounding us, and then standing behind each one of us. Again, I have the feeling that this is our lineage, our angels and guides. They don't have faces. I sense that they are entities standing behind us and working alongside. We are given presents from our angelic guides, one in our left "receiving hand" and one in our right "creative" hand.

* **Paula** receives a feather pen in her left hand and a ring with four turquoise petals and a diamond in the middle in her right.

* **Melissa** receives an ink pen in her left hand and a ring with four magenta petals and a diamond in the middle in her right.

* **Gabriel** receives letters in her left hand and a golden ring in her right.

So interesting that you two got my signature energy colors of turquoise and magenta. I think you both received my frequency, which now joins us more fully energetically. I sense that it works reciprocally, too. Gabriele and Melissa have an essence that brings Paula into the right frequency, and Gabriele and Paula have an essence that then activates the right frequency in Melissa.

New Village 22 Meditation #16: New Moon

Mediation setup: Visualize the earth light portal and feel into what can arise there or how we can access the light of this portal in order to manifest intentional community.

Melissa meditation report:
Four of us are occupying the four corners of the bottom of a pyramid. I introduce our new member Barbara to the group and we all affectionately acknowledge each other. I ask what the light coming from the earth portal is and receive: "voice (expression) of the new world." I ask what the gold ring and two petal rings from Gabriele's meditation might represent. I receive that the gold ring is truth and the petal rings facilitate communication of that truth. We are to hold truth in our hearts to facilitate blossoming.

I begin to chant until the pulsing energy from my hand chakras is quite strong. We stand up and let the magnificent light from our hearts swirl outward and upwards into the column of light, connecting us to each other's heart light. We joyfully lean in toward the light. Our feet are firmly planted on earth but the feeling is that we are soaring in this light, as if we were hang gliding on the light energy. There is no fear and no sense that we will fall into the light center. The light center is like gusts of wind that keeps us floating (think of those "wind tunnels" that simulate parachute jumping). We are laughing and enjoying this experience. When we are finished with this play, we lean back to stand straight and then sit cross legged. We give thanks from our hearts to earth, fire, water, air.

Suddenly the streaming earth light changes shape becoming a flower with light petals arching over our heads (like the rings). Intuitively I realize this earth light portal is the Earth's Heart Chakra. This is the energy we will be playing with to create the new community. We stand and rotate positions until we have each "occupied" the four corners.

Gabriele's meditation notes:

We are sitting around the triangle facing each other. The portal within the triangle allows beaming light to come forth. I suddenly see Paula "materializing" silver stars out of the beaming light. She reaches into the light separating out silver stars that she then throws to me. I catch the stars and juggle with them until they become firmer and get into some kind of shape. This not-yet-ready shape I throw over to Melissa and they change shape. This star hand-off process is very satisfying.

Second meditation:

I see us four sitting around the circular star portal with the glowing light. We don't sit in triangular shape anymore; our sitting arrangement has changed into an equal sided trapezium (or trapezoid).

Melissa, after I read your notes I realized that this shape could be the foundation of a pyramid. While looking at this sitting arrangement I receive the words "as above, so below."

I feel called to ask Gaia herself if there is anything we can know and learn from her today. I receive the words, "Breathe into the heart." I do this. "Breathe into the heart and breathe from the heart. Growth and peace evolve from the heart, expand from the heart." I keep on breathing into the heart five or six times. At this stage I regret that I didn't have a recorder, because there was so much information in words, visuals, smells, tones, tastes, textures that was amazing. Here is what I remember. I am shown people holding the shape of a heart. I ask how Gaia would like us to cooperate with her. I receive the visual of a landscape in which people live in flow with the energies of the land. Buildings and nature are hard to differentiate from each other, feels much like all natural building materials. The landscape and building feng shui is soft and gentle. The way the dwellings are arranged allow for natural energies to flow everywhere — like Earth's nourishing energies have been made visible, allowing Gaia to be in its most beautiful shape. Round might be the first materialized version/form of energy.

I receive the words, "Empowering All — not just one!" I ask about communal areas, how they might look and receive that there should be many, not just one communal area, areas that will shift and change according to its use. I sense this has to do with allowing the natural unfolding of life and I receive the sentence: "Learn in practical terms what it means to be ONE, but still be unique each of you." Also, I see colorful butterflies coming out of the portal dancing around our heads. I also ask about how Barbara complements us and receive the words "accelerator" and get the colors "turquoise and yellow" for her. It was a very beautiful meditation, the visuals and impressions went on and on.

Paula's meditation notes:

Hello all and welcome Barbara, I did my meditation outside in the evening (lovely) and it was quite simple and rather straightforward. First, the three of us were tossing a big beach ball. It was fun, but kind of awkward and we kept stopping and having to go chase the ball. We had a hard time keeping it up in the air. Then Barbara joined in and the ball got a bit smaller and changed from a typical multi-colored beach ball to a solid blue orb that pulsed with energy. It became much easier to keep it in play. Then the vision widened to (somehow) include the whole world, and I saw that there were lots of pairs, triads, foursomes and even slightly bigger groups playing with their own balls — all different colors and all pulsing. That was it. Actually it was very satisfying and left me feeling really delighted.

Barbara's meditation report:

I am standing in a labyrinth filled with lavender along a series of pathways. The fragrance fills the air; bees are busy at work collecting pollen. I then notice children playing in the center of the labyrinth; their laughter is contagious; there is light and joy in their playfulness. I could not figure out what they were doing until I walked closer to the center of the labyrinth; the place where the light was the brightest. The children were carrying baskets of fruit and vegetables and placing them upon the light as offerings of sustenance. As each basket was deposited, large roots began to grow from the bottoms that reached deep into the ground of the light; returning to the source that gave them life. The Earth, the light, the life force energy was larger and more energetic than when the plants were first harvested.

Resources:

There are so many people doing remarkable things in the world. I encourage you to set the intention to connect to such people. That alone makes all the difference in shifting global perception and energy in a positive direction. Here are resources I mention in the book, as well as a small sampling of the people and information that I have found fascinating and inspirational.

Articles:
David P. Barash, "Over Time, Buddhism and Science Agree: Understanding the impermanence of everything including ourselves," Web. 9 January 2014, http://nautil.us/issue/9/time/over-time-buddhism-and-science-agree

Damanhur® Community Blog, "Social and Economic Model," Web. 27 January 2014, http://www.damanhurblog.com/the-economic-system-of-damanhur/

Jacque Fresco, "What is a Resource Based Economy?" Web. 30 June 2012, http://www.thevenusproject.com/about/resource-based-economy

Kansas State University communications and marketing press release, "Buddhism in Second Life: Anthropologist studies spirituality in virtual reality," Web. 28 January 2013, http://www.k-state.edu/today/announcement.php?id=6732

Morley Winograd and Michael Hais, "How Millennials Could Upend Wall Street and Corporate American," Web. 31 May 2014, http://

www.brookings.edu/research/papers/2014/05/millenials-upend-wall-street-corporate-america-winograd-hais

Shoshana Zuboff, "Creating Value in the Age of Distributed Capitalism," McKinsey Quarterly, September 2010, Web. 30 April 2014 http://www.mckinsey.com/insights/strategy/creating_value_in_the_age_of_distributed_capitalism

Tom Kenyon, "The Effects of Sound on Your Innate Genius," Web. 10 January 2014, http://www.tomkenyon.com/the-effects-of-sound-on-your-innate-genius

Books:

Anderson, Joyce. *Tellaga and Conred: Rescuing Your Talents from Constant Comparing*. Bloomington, Indiana: AuthorHouse, 2012.

Andrew, Ted. *Animal Speak: The Spiritual and Magical Powers of Creatures Great and Small*. St. Paul, Minnesota: Llewellyn Publications, 2003.

Anodea, Judith. *The Global Heart Awakens: Humanity's Rite of Passage from the Love of Power to the Power of Love*. San Rafael, CA: Shift Books, 2013.

Baldwin, Christina. *Calling The Circle: The First And Future Culture*. New York, NY: Bantam Books, 1998.

Baldwin, J. *Bucky Works: Buckminster Fuller's Ideas for Today*. New York, NY: John Wiley & Sons, Inc., 1997.

Christopher, David. *The Holy Universe*. Santa Rose, CA: New Story Press, 2014.

Courtney, Hazel. *Countdown to Coherence: A Spiritual Journey Toward a Scientific Theory of Everything*. London: Watkins Publishing, 2010.

Hidalgo, Sharlyn. *The Healing Power of Trees: Spiritual Journeys Through the Celtic Tree Calendar*. Woodbury, Minnesota: Llewellyn Publications, 2010.

____. *Nazmy — Love is My Religion: Egypt, Travel and a Quest for Peace*. New York, NY: Phoenix Rising Publishing, 2014.

Kenyon, Tom. *The Hathor Material: Messages From An Ascended Civilization*. Orcas, WA: ORB Communications, 9th printing 2012.

Rene, Lucia. *Unplugging the Patriarchy: A Mystical Journey into the Heart of a New Age*. Williamsburg, Virginia: Crown Chakra Publishing, 2009.

Sklar, Marty. *Dream It! Do It! My Half-Century Creating Disney's Magic Kingdoms*. Glendale, California: Disney Editions, 2013.

St. Germain, Maureen. *Beyond The Flower of Life: Multidimensional Activation of Your Higher Self, the Inner Guru — Advanced MerKaBa Teachings*. New York: Phoenix Rising Publishing, October 26, 2009.

Websites and blogs

Adam White, http://www.davieswhite.co.uk/site/

Alan Seale, http://www.transformationalpresence.org/

Ananda Village, http://www.ananda.org/about-ananda-sangha/spiritual-communities/

Arcosanti, https://arcosanti.org/

Auroville, http://www.auroville.org/

Arthur Brock, http://emergingleaderlabs.org/

BrightCo, http://www.gobright.co

Christina Baldwin, https://www.peerspirit.com/

Context Institute, http://www.context.org

Converge, Pacific Northwest Innovation Summit, http://www.convergepnw.com

Damanhur, http://www.damanhur.org/

Darrell Toland, http://www.dtoland.com/

Erin Lee Gafill, http://www.eringafill.com/

Findhorn Ecovillage, http://www.ecovillagefindhorn.com/

Jena Griffiths, http://www.ear-thschool.com

Joyce Anderson, http://www.conversationswithyourself.com/

Karen Joy Fletcher, http://www.qidancing.com/

Linda Howe, http://akashicstudies.com/

Marci Shimoff, http://www.happyfornoreason.com/home.asp

Mary Alice Long, http://playequalspeace.com/

Nora Herold, http://noraherold.com/

Inhabitat: Design Will Save the World, http://www.inhabitat.com

Julie Umpleby, https://www.diamondlightworld.net/

Kris Steinnes, http://www.krysaliseadership.com

Kristiina Hiukka, http://kristiinahiukka.com/

Liliane Mavridara, http://www.lilianemavridara.com/

Mary Alice Long, http://www.playequalspeace.com

Maureen St. Germain, http://www.maureenstgermain.com

O.U.R Ecovillage, http://ourecovillage.org/about/our-history-and-development/

Pippa Biddle, http://www.pippabiddle.com

Raja Choudhury, Spirituality and Consciousness, https://www.linke-din.com/groups/Spirituality-Consciousness-152776/about

Sarah Varcas, Intuitive Astrology for Heart and Soul, http://astro-awakenings.co.uk/

Suzanne Anderson, http://koreevolution.com/

William Meader, http://www.emergentlight.com

Wendy Kennedy, http://www.higherfrequencies.net/

Woman in Innovation, http://www.womenininnovation.org

Women of Wisdom, http://www.womenofwisdom.org

Zen Gardner, http://www.zengardner.com/

Video/movies:
Adam White, *Dinton Pastures Nature Play Space — Opening Day with Amber Hill & Davies White Landscape Architects, web 19 May 2014,* *http://youtu.be/MVrUnk8W9Kg*

Kirsten Dirksen, *Medieval Spanish ghost town becomes self-sufficient,* Web. 8 July 2013, http://youtu.be/91pBFyLWIx4

Logan LaPlante, *Hackschooling makes me happy: Logan LaPlante at TEDxUniversity ofNevada,* Web. 13 February 2013, http://youtu.be/h11u3vtcpaY

Mark Boyle, *TEDxO'Porto - Mark Boyle - The Moneyless Man,* http://tedxtalks.ted.com/video/TEDxOPorto-Mark-Boyle-The-Money

Nikki Silva, *There's No Place Like Here: Communal living with Nikki Silva,* Web. 10 September 2013, http://youtu.be/fyeaTLi3EsI

Paul Wimbush, *Living in the Future (EcoVillages) — Tinker's Bubble.* Off-grid eco community in Somerset, England. Web. 12 July 2014, http://youtu.be/Fag4PowX4bU

Raja Choudhury, *The Quantum Indians,* http://youtu.be/7z9NUV_YrO0

Ward Serril, *Song of the New Earth: Tom Kenyon and the Power of Sound,* Woody Creek Pictures, May 2014, http://woodycreekpictures.com/films/song-of-the-new-earth/

New Village 22
member biographies:

Melissa Wadsworth is a new-community visionary, intuitive creative, dream coach, speaker and author. Melissa has dedicated her life to exploring consciousness, creativity, the meaning in all experience, and supporting people worldwide in their life journeys. An avid student of life, she aims for a vibration of easy exuberance in all that she does. Her path has encompassed a career in public relations, the creation of an essential oil-based face and body product line, teaching her intuitive dream board process, and intuitive artistry. http://www.melissawadsworth.com

Gabriele Neumann is an expert in energy and change processes, and a property investor and manager. For 10 years she worked with blue chip corporations to facilitate change, including management of human resources, organizational development, change management responsiveness, development of human potential and personnel assessment. Since 2000 Gabriele has worked with the energy dynamics of places and buildings based on her knowledge of remote energy healing, constellation work and geomancy. Gabriele combines these methods with her intuitive abilities in the Eartheart Matters™ process which addresses the energetic and emotional blocks connected or stored up in a building, piece of land, home, rental, business premises or any other space that is causing an undesired effect. http://wwww.eartheartliving.com

Paula Russell believes in lifelong learning and has taught classes in a variety of settings for people of all ages in everything from botany and chemistry, to art history, the magic of math, thinking, Shakespeare, Latin, writing and more. She leads art and culture tours to Italy, and messes around with paints, plays congas in an Afro-Latino percussion group, and reads way too much.

Barbara Krauss is a steward of creative inquiry. Her work is an organic blend of creativity coaching, inspirational teaching, motivational speaking, leading workshops and holding the space as a spiritual guide. She is most alive when immersed in creative expression, whether it is through movement, art or writing. Barbara shares her passion and playful spirit as a Certified Master Kaizen-Muse™ Creativity Coach, licensed Nia Instructor, ARTbundance™ Coach and Practitioner, adjunct faculty for Kore Evolution™, and owner of The Centre for Organic YESipes™. Barbara has a BA in Fine Arts and Psychology with specialization in American Sign Language and Art Therapy. She is a graduate of Kore Leadership™ Women's "Integral Leadership Advanced Leadership Development Program. http://www.barbarakrauss.com.

Made in the USA
San Bernardino, CA
10 September 2019